The Ultimate Memory Book

Remember <u>Anything</u>
Quickly & Easily

By Robert Sandstrom

stepping
stone
books

Manufactured in the United States of America.

Publisher's Cataloging in Publication Data

Sandstrom, Robert I.
The Ultimate Memory Book.

Bibliography: p. 157-158.

1. Mnemonics.   I.   Title.
BF385   154.1   90-70923
ISBN   0-9626918-5-2

For information or quantity discounts, contact:

Stepping Stone Books
P.O. Box 33308
Granada Hills, CA 91394-0045
Phone (818) 368-4268

This book is dedicated to my parents
Bob & Mary Sandstrom,
with all my love

CONTENTS

INTRODUCTION

In learning the material presented in this book you will increase your memory capabilities as much as 500%! The systems and techniques are tried and proven—they are ultimately powerful yet simple and easy to learn. You will see amazing results in a very short time.

The chapters

The first chapter contains a series of tests that will help determine your *present* memory capabilities. Your score will act as a benchmark by which you will measure your improvements. Chapters "Two" through "Six" cover the memory principles and techniques that are fundamental to all "Memory-Systems." Chapters "Seven" through "Seventeen" contain "Memory-Systems" ranging from basic to more advanced. These "Systems" show you how to:

1. remember phone-numbers, and dates—the very first time you hear them...
2. remember the names and faces of everyone you meet...
3. get *better* grades and test scores with *less* study time...
4. learn vocabulary words and foreign languages—with ease...
5. memorize weekly appointments & schedules...
6. solve any and every memory problem...and much, much more!

(*Many examples and exercises have been provided to help you absorb and apply each system.*) Chapter "Eighteen" will teach you how to cure absentmindedness—for good! Chapter "Nineteen" covers powerful new study techniques that will enable you to learn faster and recall more. Chapter "Twenty" shows you how to use the memory systems and techniques to memorize magazines and books! Chapters "Twenty-One" through "Twenty-Three" are bonus systems. These systems will enable you to memorize the calendar and speeches. You will also learn how to easily expand and increase the power of previous systems.

How to get the most from this book

Each chapter builds on the one before it. If you wish to attain maximum results you should study each chapter in succession—don't skip around. Make sure you understand and can apply the material in a chapter before moving on to the next. This book should not be read passively.

Take it to the limit

If a weight-lifter wishes to build bigger muscles, he must push himself to lift more weight than he could previously, thereby becoming stronger and more agile. You can build a stronger and faster memory by pushing yourself each time you use the memory systems and techniques. Once you've learned them, force yourself to execute them faster than you did before. By doing so you will expand your mental boundaries. You'll be amazed at what you can do if you only try.

The power to remember is within all of us. This book will teach you how to unleash that power and remember more than you ever dreamed possible!

CHAPTER 1

HOW WELL DO YOU REMEMBER?

In this chapter we will test your *present* memory capabilities. I stress "present" because your memory capabilities will change dramatically as you learn the material in this book.

At this stage, some of the tests might seem difficult or even impossible. Don't let that worry you. We are merely establishing a tangible means by which you will measure your improvements—and vast improvements they will be! The test scores do not reflect your memory *capacity*, only your *present memory capabilities*. After you learn the memory Systems and Techniques, come back and take the tests again—prove to yourself just how powerful your memory really is.

Find a comfortable place where you won't be interrupted and take the tests. You will need to have a clock with a second-hand in order to time yourself. Be sure to keep within the time limits of each test and score yourself accurately. **NOTE**: *You don't have to complete all of the tests in one sitting.*

TEST 1

Read the following list of items and try to memorize them in any order. Take 2 minutes to do so. Start now.

1. **Key**
2. **Watermelon**
3. **Pencil**
4. **Tooth-Brush**
5. **Clock**
6. **Handkerchief**
7. **Bicycle**
8. **Hunger**
9. **Strawberry**
10. **Blimp**
11. **Roller-Skates**
12. **Paper-Clip**
13. **Coffee**
14. **Stamp**
15. **Wrench**
16. **Happiness**
17. **Candy Bar**
18. **Foot**
19. **Pin**
20. **Dog**

Turn to the next page and fill in your answers.

TEST 1 RESPONSES

Without looking at the list of items, write down as many items as you remembered.

1.
2.
3.
4.
5.
6.
7.
8.
9.
10.
11.
12.
13.
14.
15.
16.
17.
18.
19.
20.

Give yourself 1 point for every item recalled. Maximum Points = 20.

Total _____18_____

TEST 2

Read the following list of twenty items and try to remember the items and the *order* in which they are given. Take no more than 2 minutes to do so.

1. Saucer
2. Cucumber
3. Tea
4. Prison
5. Table
6. Bat
7. Furnace
8. Sunshine
9. Banana
10. Horse
11. Eye Lash
12. Magazine
13. Nail
14. Elastic
15. South
16. Gate
17. Ice
18. Helmet
19. Cough Drop
20. Lake

Turn to the next page and fill in your answers.

TEST 2 RESPONSES

Without looking at the list of items, write down as many items as you remembered in their correct order.

1.
2.
3.
4.
5.
6.
7.
8.
9.
10.
11.
12.
13.
14.
15.
16.
17.
18.
19.
20.

Give yourself 1 point for every item recalled and 1 point for every item in its correct position. Maximum Points = 40.

Total ___24___

TEST 3

Memorize the name that goes with the occupation. Take no more than two minutes to do so. Start now.

Bill Murphy	Police Officer
Robert Atleman	Janitor
Peter Wingwright	Dentist
Nancy Patterson	Film Editor
Paul Friedman	Accountant
Steven Mitchell	Tailor
Brian Manchester	Mechanic
Judy Blum	Teacher

TEST 3 RESPONSES

Without looking at the list above, write in the name that goes with the occupation.

Janitor _____

Dentist _____

Tailor _____

Police Officer _____

Mechanic _____

Teacher _____

Film Editor _____

Accountant _____

Give yourself 1 point for every correct answer. Maximum Points = 8.

Total _____ $4\frac{1}{2}$

TEST 4

Below, are six 15-digit numbers. Take 30 seconds to memorize each number. After the first 30 seconds, cover up the number and write it down as best you can in the space below. Continue in the same manner for the remaining numbers. Start now.

1. 374658271994369
2. 279832541674480
3. 896483720689467
4. 495079117392601
5. 230951026360714
6. 452735488525972

TEST 4 RESPONSES

Write each 15-digit number in the following spaces.

1. _____
2. _____
3. _____
4. _____
5. _____
6. _____

Give yourself 1 point for every number correctly recalled. Each digit must have been given in its correct order. Maximum Points = 6.

Total _____

TEST 5

Below, is a list of ten people and their telephone numbers. Take no more than four minutes to memorize the phone numbers and the people they belong to. Start now.

1. The optometrist	788-0699
2. The butcher	852-1910
3. The police	434-7831
4. The country club	535-6386
5. Your partner	368-1465
6. The movie theater	944-8128
7. Your hair stylist	232-1947
8. The pet clinic	669-7336
9. Your piano teacher	336-7441
10. The drug store	878-1942

Turn to the next page and fill in your answers.

TEST 5 RESPONSES

Fill in the proper phone number for each person.

Your hair stylist   _____
The pet clinic   _____
The optometrist   _____
The butcher   _____
Your piano teacher   _____
The drug store   _____
The country club   _____
Your partner   _____
The police   _____
The movie theater   _____

Give yourself 2 points for each correct number recalled. Maximum Points = 20.

Total ___2___

TEST 6

Memorize the following list of appointments. Take no more than 90 seconds to do so. Start now.

Thursday 1:00 P.M. : Pick up papers from lawyer.
Monday 10:00 A.M. : Meet with labor group
Friday 3:30 P.M. : Pick up flyers from printer
Tuesday 9:15 A.M. : Drop off proposal
Thursday 11:45 A.M. : Dentist appointment
Wednesday 7:30 P.M. : Singing lesson

TEST 6 RESPONSES

Cover the above schedule and recall as many appointments as possible. Write them in the space below; start with Monday and continue through Friday.

Give yourself 1 point for each correct appointment recalled.
Maximum Points = 6.

Total ___2___

You have completed your initial testing. Add your test scores and put the total in the space next to Grand Total. Maximum Points = 100.

Grand Total _50.5_

The average score, for a person with an *un-trained memory*, falls between 10 and 50 points. The same people who initially scored between 10 and 50 points scored between 95 and 100 points after they learned the material taught in this book. That's exciting! You, too, will be excited as you learn to unleash the memory-power that lies within you.

NOTE: *In learning the techniques that follow, you should pace yourself; give yourself time to digest each technique. Study each chapter in succession for each builds on the one before it.*

CHAPTER 2

BASIC MEMORY INGREDIENTS

The "Basic Memory Ingredients" are fundamental to all memory techniques. You need to understand and know how to use them if you wish to develop a super-power memory. Keep that in mind as you read this chapter.

Association
Imagination

Association is the process of connecting new information to what we already know. Therefore, if we wish to memorize something, we must associate it with something that is firm in our memory. For example, in music, the spaces of the treble clef are f, a, c, and e. To most people, these are random abstract letters. Abstract things are difficult to remember. But, if we *associate* the letters with something we already know, we can memorize them easily. The letters f-a-c-e spell FACE. Now that you've associated these letters with something you know, FACE, they are easy to remember.

Imagination plays a dual role in memorization. We use imagination to strengthen our associations and to transform ordinary images into extra-ordinary images. Extra-ordinary things are easy to remember; ordinary things are not. For example, if you think back to the 1988 World Series you probably won't remember who struck out; but you *will* remember Kirk Gibson's *extra*-ordinary winning home run! Most people know exactly where they were the day they got news of John F. Kennedy's assassination; how many people could tell you where they were the day before it happened? Extra-ordinary things stick in our memory. Therefore, if we wish to remember something ordinary, we simply imagine it in some extra-ordinary way; then *associate* it with something we already know. Lets try it.

The word "**feint**" means: *a false attack*

Picture yourself talking to an old man. All of a sudden his *false* teeth jump right out of his mouth and start *attack*ing you. As a result you **faint**. We have now made an extra-ordinary story out of an ordinary word and definition. When we hear or see the word "feint," we associate it with *faint*ing as the result of a *false* teeth *attack*. Imagination is the key to a powerful memory.

We all posses a good imagination

You may be thinking to yourself, "I don't have a good imagination!" Truth is, you do have a good imagination, you just haven't been using it lately!

Think about it. Do you know a child who doesn't posses a good imagination? I don't. As children, it's natural to imagine or conjure up wild images and stories; society advocates it. Unfortunately, as we get older we are told "Stop dreaming and get down to business." And that is precisely what we do—we stop exercising our creative mind and quell our imaginative powers.

Have no fear, the creative brain lingers in all of us. It's sitting back there just waiting to be used. All we have to do is exercise it back into shape. You will do this *automatically* whenever you use the memory techniques. The more you use them, the sharper your imaginative skills will become.

Memory Aids

We remember with all our senses: sight, sound, touch, taste, and smell. Therefore, we should include (in our mental pictures) as many of them as we can. How many times have you *smelled* something that elicits memories from long ago? When we *hear* a violin we know it's a violin because we remember what a violin *sounds* like. When we *see* an old friend, we recognize him because we remember what he *looks* like. The more senses we use to remember something, the easier it will be to remember!

In order to remember "well," you should include the following memory-aids in your mental pictures. You don't need to use all of them in every picture but you *must* use at least a few.

Sight
Sound
Touch
Smell
Taste
Color   (it is *extremely* helpful to use color in your images)

(Memory-Aids continued)

Size   (make things much larger or much smaller)

Absurdity   (the more ridiculous, the better)

Exaggeration

Action   (you must include as much action as possible)

Sensuality   (use your imagination)

Quantity   (picture hundreds or thousands of the same item)

Pictures, the clearer the better!

Psychologists say, "Our body cannot tell the difference between what is real and what is imagined." This is true. If you vividly picture something in your mind, your body will react as if you were *really* doing or seeing it. I remember reading a book about the subconscious mind and it demonstrated this phenomenon with an experiment. I'd like to try it with you. Use your imagination and all your senses as you read the following paragraph:

"Picture a fresh lemon. See the bright yellow color. You are holding the lemon in your hand and can feel its texture. You can feel the skin and its nooks and buds. Now picture putting the lemon up to your nose and smelling it. You can smell its distinctive fragrance. Imagine that you take a knife and cut the lemon in half. You can feel the knife cutting through it. You can see the juice running on to the table. When you pick the lemon up again, you feel the juice in your hand. Imagine yourself putting the lemon back up to your nose and smelling it again. The fragrance is even stronger than before. Now, imagine opening your mouth and taking a big bite of the lemon!"

At the point when you bit into the lemon (if you were vividly seeing, feeling, smelling and tasting it) your mouth should have been filled with saliva. That's proof that our body does react to what is *imagined* in the same way as it reacts to what is *real*. This is why people under hypnosis develop blisters on their skin when told they are being burned with something. The hypnotist, merely touching a subject with his finger, creates the reaction when the subject truly believes or imagines he is being touched by a hot iron. The body is reacting to something *imagined*, not real.

A boy riding slowly through a park on a bicycle suddenly notices he is being chased by a bear. The bicyclist senses danger! His adrenaline starts to flow heavily and his heart begins to pump faster as he breaks out in a sweat. He pedals his bike as fast as he can. When he looks back, the bear has stopped. In fact, it wasn't a bear at all—it was a friend dressed in a bear costume. He was tricked! The point is, what he saw wasn't *real* but he *imagined* it was. His body reacted to something that was *imagined*!

When we see, feel, touch, taste, or smell something, that sensation or image is encoded into our memory. Then, when we want to remember it, our brain decodes it and puts a mental picture of it in our mind. If what we originally experienced was *vivid*, the picture in our mind will be vivid. If what we experienced was *vague*, the picture in our mind will be vague. In other words, what goes in is what comes back out. When we *imagine* something vividly, we are encoding or recording that image into our memory. Our brain is therefore able to reproduce a vivid image of what we need to recall. If the initial image is vague, it will be reproduced in a vague way and will not be distinguishable.

The point to all of this is that a vivid, crystal-clear image is recallable. Therefore, when you visualize, do it vividly!

The exercise below will give you some practice using vivid visualization. I would like you to read through and visualize the story. Pay close attention to the details. For example; You will see the word "shovel" in the story. When you picture it in your mind, see it as vividly and clearly as possible. What kind of shovel is it? Is it long or is it short? Is it shiny and new or is it old and rusty? Does it have a handle? Is the shovel itself rectangular or is it shaped like a spade? Is it heavy or is it light? When you visualize in detail, you firmly implant the image into your memory. Another image you will see is a "Yellow Volkswagen." Is the car in good shape or is it banged up? Is the color a shinny yellow or is it dull? Is it missing any hubcaps? Is it a convertible or a bug? If you were *physically* looking at a Volkswagen, you would automatically know if it is a bug or a convertible; old or new; dented or not dented; because you see a clear picture of it. You must learn to see mental pictures with your *mind's* eye, in the same way as you see real pictures with your real eyes. At first, vivid visualization may seem difficult but that's only because you are not used to doing it. In time, with a little practice it will become automatic. You will see vivid images as quickly as if you were physically looking at them.

In the following story there are 20 key-words in *italics*. As you read it, take some time to vividly picture each key-word image. See the colors, smell the smells, feel the feelings, and hear the sounds.

Circus Story

"You are at a *circus*. Up on a *tightrope* is a *monkey*. In the monkey's right hand is a *shovel* and in his left hand is an *apple pie*. The monkey begins to eat the pie with the shovel and loses his balance. He drops the pie, which falls onto a big *black elephant*. The elephant becomes scarred and runs out into the *parking lot*. He jumps onto the roof of a *yellow*

Volkswagen that is being driven by a *Doberman Pincer* who is wearing a *tuxedo* and smoking a *cigar*. The dog stops the car, reaches into the *glove box* and pulls out a *gun*. He gets out of the car and shoots the elephant. A nearby *police officer* hears the shot and comes running over. He is wearing nothing but a pair of *brown leather loafers*. He ties the dog up to a *fire hydrant* with a *white extension cord* then carries the injured elephant to a *hospital*. The doctor removes the bullet with a pair of *rusty pliers*, places a two foot *band-aid* on the elephant's wound, and sends him back to the circus."

Exercise

From memory, fill the missing key-words in the spaces below. When you have finished, check your answers against the list that follows.

"You are at a _____. Up on a _____ is a _____. In his right hand is a _____ and in his left hand is an _____. He begins to eat the — with the — and loses his balance. He drops the — which falls onto a big _____. The — becomes scarred and runs out into the _____. He jumps onto the roof of a _____ that is being driven by a _____ who is wearing a _____ and smoking a _____. The dog stops the car, reaches into the _____ and pulls out a _____. He gets out of the car and shoots the —. A nearby _____ hears the shot and comes running over. He is wearing nothing but a pair of _____. He ties the dog up to a _____ with a _____ then carries the injured — to a _____. The

27

doctor removes the bullet with a pair of _____,
places a two foot _____ on the wound, and
sends the — back to the circus."

Key-words from Circus Story

1. Circus	11. Cigar
2. Tight Rope	12. Glove Box
3. Monkey	13. Gun
4. Shovel	14. Police Officer
5. Apple Pie	15. Brown Leather Loafers
6. Black Elephant	16. Fire Hydrant
7. Parking Lot	17. White Extension Cord
8. Yellow Volkswagen	18. Hospital
9. Doberman Pincer	19. Rusty Pliers
10. Tuxedo	20. Band-Aid

Did you remember each item in detail? Did you remember the color of the extension cord or the kind of pie the monkey was holding? Did you remember that the pliers were rusty or that the brown loafers were made of leather? If you didn't, your pictures weren't vivid enough. The purpose of this exercise is to stress the importance of detail and clarity. I want you to get into the habit of forming vivid images because the clearer the picture, the easier it will be to recall. By the way, give yourself a pat on the back; you just remembered most, if not all of a list of 20 items!

Lets put the "Basic Memory Ingredients" to work now by learning "THE LINK". . .

CHAPTER 3

THE LINK

The first and most basic memory technique I will teach you is called "The Link." You can use the link to memorize lists of items such as "Shopping Lists" or "To Do Lists." It is also used in conjunction with many other memory techniques you will learn.

Linking is fun and easy to do. You simply make a connection between two unrelated items by forming a ridiculous picture that associates them to each-other. (The more absurd the picture, the better.) Once you've linked "item 1" to "item 2," you can form another picture that links "item 2" to "item 3" and another that links "item 3" to "item 4" and so on. You are in effect chaining each item together. As a result, the list of items will be easy to remember because each item will remind you what comes after it!

We will use "The Link" and the "Basic Memory Ingredients" to help us memorize the list of items on the following page.

ITEM LIST

Tree
Change-Purse
Rope
Car
Sky
Pencil
Doctor
Horse
Gum
Blanket

Let's link *tree* to *change-purse:* Imagine a giant **tree** that has **change-purses** (instead of fruit) growing off it. (See the colors of the leaves and branches; See the branches bending because the change purses are heavy. See the shiny brass rims on the purses; How would it feel to reach up and pluck a change-purse off the tree? See yourself doing it!)

Now let's link *change-purse* to *rope:* You open your **change-purse** and pull out a **rope**. To your surprise the rope keeps coming and coming. You have pulled miles of rope from your little change-purse. (Feel yourself opening the change-purse; Feel the texture of the rope; See the color of the rope; See the piles of rope on the ground.)

Rope to *car:* Picture making a lasso out of a piece of **rope**. Now picture yourself standing in the street and when a **car** passes by, you lasso it. When the rope catches, the car drags you down the street. (See your images CLEARLY!)

Car to *sky:* You look up and see hundreds of **car**s dangling in the **sky** by chains that reach up through the clouds. They are smashing against each-other in the wind. You can see windshields cracking and mirrors falling etc.

Sky to *pencil:* It's raining **pencils** by the thousands. See thousands of pencils falling from the **sky**. (See and hear them bouncing off the ground.)

Pencil to *doctor:* Your **doctor** is giving you a shot with a **pencil**! He is jabbing the pencil into your arm. (See the lead of the pencil sticking into your arm. Feel how painful it is. See the color of the pencil.)

Doctor to *horse:* You're at the race track and the **horses** are being ridden by fully dressed **doctors**! You can see their stethoscopes bouncing around as they race down the track.

Horse to *gum:* Picture a **horse** chewing a huge wad of **gum**. He then blows a giant bubble and it pops; it sticks all over his face.

Gum to *blanket:* Instead of covering yourself with a **blanket** you take a giant piece of chewed **gum** and stretch it out to the size of a blanket and cover yourself with it. (Sticky!)

Now, without looking at the list, write down the items you remember on a separate piece of paper.

Congratulate yourself. I'm sure you remembered most if not all of them. Did you notice how one item reminded you of the next item, and how that item reminded you of what came after it? That is what *linking* is all about. You "chain" all the items together. It is possible to link hundreds of items into one long chain. All you need to do is see your images *clearly*, and your memory will take care of the rest.

HINT: If you had a problem remembering the first item on the list, simply think of any item near the beginning of the list and work backward. You'll eventually come to the first item.

If you wish to retain a list of items over a long period of time you must mentally review at intervals that work best for you. You will need to experiment to find what works best. I suggest reviewing (the list you wish to remember) three times, the first day. Each review should be a few hours apart. On the second day, review twice about 8 hours apart. Then review a couple of days after that and maybe a week after that. At that time, the list should be knowledge. In other words, you'll remember the items without having to think of the crazy pictures. Every person is different, therefore, you should review in a way that works best for you. Reviewing doesn't take long. (Although *reading* the descriptions takes a while, you can summons up the images in just seconds.)

Exercise

The images created when linking or making associations are much more powerful when they are *your own*. Make up a list of ten words and memorize them.

CHAPTER 4

WORD SUBSTITUTION

Names of people and places usually cannot be pictured in our minds—they are abstract, and we have trouble picturing abstract things. With word substitution, we can take an abstract word and change it into a three dimensional picture. Abstract words become easy to deal with when they are turned into pictures because our brain thinks in pictures. For example; the name Makowski would be hard to remember in itself but if you pictured your **Ma** on a **Cow** that is **Skiing** down a hill, it would be very easy to remember. Ma, cow, ski,— Makowski. It would be hard to picture the word Minnesota but it would be easy to picture a **mini-soda**.

After an abstract word is changed into a picture it can be easily associated or linked to something else.

Rules for word substitution

1. Break down the word into syllables by **sound** not spelling.

2. Make a clear descriptive picture out of each syllable.

3. If a particular syllable does not form a picture on its own then combine it with the next syllable. You might have to combine 2 or 3 syllables to get a picture.

4. Sometimes a word and all its syllables will not translate into a picture. You then must form a picture that is representative or symbolic of it. Example, the word relaxation, re - lax - a - shun, is not picturable either as a whole or in part. In this case, we could represent the word relaxation with a picture of a **rocking-chair**. (You should choose a picture that best represents the word to *you*; For example; you might choose **fishing-pole** to represent relaxation instead of rocking chair.) Symbolic pictures are not as good as sound-alike pictures but, sometimes we have no choice but to use them.

Let's turn the following abstract words into pictures following the rules for word substitution.

1. Titanic

Ti tan ic　We can picture **tie** and we can picture **tan** but can we picture **ic**? You might picture ic as "ick", as in blah, "I don't like it, ick!" But "ick" isn't tangible so we should avoid it if possible. Another choice might be **ink**, (ic - ink). Ink sounds like ic and it is a picture word; we can link it to tie and tan. To remember Titanic you would simply picture a *tie* that is *tan* in color and has a big *ink* stain on it. Don't worry about ink not reminding you of ic. Your true memory will take care of that for you.

2. Voracious

Vor a cious　We can substitute **four** for *vor* and we can substitute **hay** for *a* and then **chess** for *cious*. That would work but it would be simpler to combine the syllables *a* and *cious* to get **aces**, acious - aces. We could then picture *four aces*. Voracious - Four Aces. (You should break a word down in a way that is simple and easy for *you* to remember. Ten people might come up with ten different word substitutions for the same word.)

3. Patriotism

Pa tri o tis m   We could substitute **pay** for *pa* and we could substitute **tree** for *tri* but, the remaining three syllables are abstract even when we combine them. They don't lend themselves to being pictured. In this case we must choose a picture word to symbolize patriotism. We might use **flag** or **marine** or even **eagle** to represent patriotism. You should choose a word that *you* can relate to—that way it will be more meaningful.

The act of breaking down words into pictures automatically forces you to focus your attention on, and become aware of the very thing you are trying to remember. This alone will aid you tremendously in remembering.

Word substitution works hand in hand with other memory techniques so it is a good idea to get some practice doing it. A dictionary is an obvious resource. Pick out words at random and break them down into pictures. You'll find the more you do it, the easier it will become. At the same time, you will be exercising your imagination and that will help in all areas of memory.

Before you go on to the next chapter, complete the exercise below.

Exercise
Turn the words on the following page into pictures using the rules for word substitution.

1. Carburetor
2. Extortion
3. Wonderful
4. Maniac (Hint: substitute May Pole for ma)
5. Detergent (You might have to use a symbolic picture)
6. Cartilage
7. Prognosticate
8. Fluent

CHAPTER 5

ENGLISH AND FOREIGN VOCABULARY

As we have learned, word substitution is an extremely powerful memory technique. It enables us to transform ordinary, two-dimensional, abstract things into colorful pictures. That is important because our mind stores information in pictures not words. For example; If I were to ask you to describe your dog to me you might say, "Well, he's brown, about 3 feet tall, and has long floppy ears." As you were describing him, you were not visualizing the **words** *brown*, *3 feet tall*, and *floppy ears*. Instead, you were seeing a **picture** of the dog in your mind and as you were picturing him, you described him to me. If I asked you to describe your house, you would do it in the same manner; you would first see a **picture** of it, then go on to describe it. You would not see an actual list of words that described it! It's a fact, *our brain stores information in pictures, not words*.

As children, we are taught to add and subtract with oranges, apples, or objects of some kind; e.g., "If I have two apples and took one away, how many would I have left?" As the words are spoken the parent or teacher removes one apple. The child is then able to **see** one apple! *We learn with pictures*.

Signs that used to read "NO SMOKING" now have a picture of a cigarette with an X going through it. Why? Because *pictures are universal, everybody understands them*. It makes sense to use pictures to help us remember.

Normally, if you wanted to remember a list of words and translations, you would repeat them over, and over, and over again until they finally sunk in. Memorizing this way can be time consuming and boring (to say the least). Instead, we can use Word Substitution to help us memorize vocabulary words and their meanings. This method is a lot quicker and a lot more fun. All you have to do is turn a meaningless word into a three-dimensional picture and link that picture to its definition. Sometimes, a definition might not be picturable; use word substitution to change it into a picture and you're all set. **NOTE:** In a previous chapter we used linking to memorize a whole list of items; now we will use it to link words to their definitions. Here are a few examples:

In French, the word *livre* means book. *Livre* sounds like "liver." We will substitute "liver" for *livre*, and link it to book. Picture yourself reading a piece of **liver** instead of a book. Now when you see or hear *livre* you will automatically think **liver.** The absurd image of reading a piece of liver instead of a book will immediately pop into you head; you'll know that *livre* means book. *Père* means father. *Père* sounds like "pear." We will substitute "pear" for *père*, and link it to father. Picture your father eating a giant **pear** that is six-feet tall. He's got both arms wrapped around it! The next time you see *père* you will think pear and see your father eating a giant one; you'll know *père* means father. *Cheval* means horse. Cheval sounds like "shovel." We will substitute "shovel" for *cheval*, and link it to horse. Picture yourself at a horse race and the jockeys are riding **shovels** instead of horses.

In Spanish, *cielo means* sky. Picture looking up and seeing millions of **cellos** (cielo) dangling around in the sky. *Escalera* means ladder. Picture yourself at a mall that uses ladders instead of **escalators** (escalera). You can see people climbing them to get to the second level.

If you tried to see any of these ridiculous pictures you will remember the translations for each word.

Test yourself:

1. Livre   *means* _____
2. Père   *means* _____
3. Cheval   *means* _____
4. Cielo   *means* _____
5. Escalera   *means* _____

If you missed any, go back and strengthen the association; then test yourself again. I'm sure you'll get them the second time.

In English, the word "appease" means to soothe or pacify. Picture a baby crying and instead of giving it a *pacifier* (pacify) you give it a dish **of peas**. Of peas sounds like appease. (Get that image into your head.) *Magnate* means rich, powerful, or very successful business person. Picture a business man in a suit; he is holding a huge powerful **magnet**. You can see millions of dollars being pulled through the air by the magnet and the money is sticking to it. He's rich! *Chagrin* means embarrassed disappointment. Imagine you go for your dentist appointment but you're an hour late. The dentist says, "I'm sorry but I can't take you."

You say, "I'm *embarrassed* because I missed *dis appoint-ment*" and the dentist **chair grin**s at you. (I know this stuff sounds crazy but it works!)

Test yourself:

1. Appease   *means* _____
2. Magnate   *means* _____
3. Chagrin   *means* _____

Again, if you missed any, go back and strengthen the association.

The examples above were provided to give you an idea of how you can use word substitution and linking to memorize all kinds of English and Foreign vocabulary words. Using this method, it is possible to learn a foreign language in a short amount of time. You can learn hundreds of vocabulary words easily by applying these systems. There is no word long or short, English or Foreign, that can't be broken down into a picture or represented by a symbolic picture. Once you've got a picture, you're all set.

We are just beginning to scratch the surface with these *basic* memory techniques. In the chapters to come, we will be learning techniques that will enable us to accomplish incredible memory feats.

CHAPTER 6

MENTAL FILING WITH "THE PEG"

Picture in your mind, an office; in the office are ten file cabinets; in the file cabinets are folders that contain important client information. The folders are listed in alphabetical order therefore, if you wanted to find Mr. Johnson's file you would look under "J." You would look under "S" to find Mr. Smith's file. It wouldn't take long to retrieve a file because they're in alphabetical order and you'd know right where to look.

Now let's assume that someone came into your office and took all the folders out of your file cabinets, put them on the ground in a big pile and mixed them up. If you now needed to locate Mr. Smith's file you'd be in trouble! Let's say you had a meeting to attend in five minutes and you needed to bring Mr.Smith's file along with you. Forget it! His file is lost amongst thousands of other files. If you were to search through the pile for it you would never make your meeting in time, in fact, you'd probably miss it all together. Why— because the information you wanted was *"mis-filed."* It was not available to you when you needed it. Of course Mr.Smith's file is there somewhere, but who cares? You needed it for your meeting but couldn't locate it.

Our memory is like a file cabinet. We put information into it just like we put information into an ordinary file cabinet. Needless to say, our mental file cabinet is infinitely larger. In fact, everything we have ever heard, seen, touched, smelled, or tasted is stored somewhere in our memory. That may sound hard to believe but it's true. That's the good news.

The bad news is that most of the information stored in our memory is *"mis-filed,"* just like the files lying on the floor in your office! Again, all the information is in there somewhere, but it is not readily accessible. As it would be difficult to locate a particular file from the pile on the floor, it is difficult to retrieve *mis-filed* information from your memory.

Case in point:

A student studies for a test, goes to school and takes the test. He comes to a question pertaining to something that was covered in class just two days before, and gets stuck. He tries hard to remember. He thinks to himself, " I know the answer to this question, we just covered this in class two days ago. Come on, what is it?" He thinks, and thinks, but can't remember. When the class is over he hands in his paper. As he is walking out of the classroom what do you think pops into his head? The *answer*!

The point is the answer was there all along, it was just *mis-filed*. Had the information been filed properly, it would have been easily recalled—he would have remembered it when he *needed* to.

This sort of thing goes on every day—you meet someone on the street that you were introduced to recently and can't remember his name. You feel uncomfortable because he remembers yours and you would like to address him with his. Ten minutes after he walks away, you remember it! The name was there all along, but it was *mis-filed*.

What we need is a "Mental Filing System" to help us *properly* file information into our memory.

I would like you to picture a wooden peg on a wall. It is a permanent part of the wall. If you hung your coat on this peg and came back to it a few hours later it would still be there. Seeing as the peg is a *permanent* part of the wall and you know right where it is, whatever you store on it will always be there and can easily be found.

What if you had a *mental* peg that worked the same way? You could *hang* information on it and retrieve it instantly, whenever you wished, because you'd know right where to go to find it! Well I've got some good news for you. Not only can you have one mental peg, you can have lists of them. Literally thousands of places to store new information that can be retrieved instantly! That's exciting!

What is a mental peg?

A mental peg is a word that is memorized—it is a *permanent* part of your memory. You can link *new* information to that peg-word by forming a ridiculous picture that associates it with the new information. To recall the new information just think of the peg-word and it will automatically remind you of it.

Peg-words are memorized in lists. The words in a peg-list are designed in a way that will make them easy to remember. In the following chapter you will learn the "Number-Shape" system. It is a peg-list consisting of ten peg-words. Once you memorize them, you can use them for the rest of your life.

When you link new information to a peg you are forcing yourself to focus all your attention on the very thing you wish to remember. This intense focusing of attention is precisely what enables us to remember. We normally don't focus so carefully.

Once you've linked information to a peg it will quickly become knowledge. Since knowledge is information you can't forget (such as your name), you will no longer need the peg to remember it. That peg will then be free to hold *new* information. The cycle goes on, and on.

Each memory system you will learn has a specific function so please don't skim past any of them. As you will see, they all work hand-in-hand!

Let's turn to the next chapter and learn the "Number-Shape" system.

CHAPTER 7

THE NUMBER-SHAPE SYSTEM

With this system, all you need to do is think of images for each of the numbers from 1 to 10. Each image should have the same *shape* as the number it represents. For example, my image for the number 2 is *swan* because 2 is *shaped* like a swan.

You can make up your own images or use any of the suggested images below. Write your choices on the following page.

NUMBERS "NUMBER-SHAPE" IMAGES

1 .... Pencil, pen, telephone-pole, candle
2 .... Swan, goose, pelican, turkey
3 .... Breasts, fanny, hills
4 .... Sailboat
5 .... Saxophone, fish-hook

NUMBERS "NUMBER-SHAPE" IMAGES

6.................	Cherry, pipe
7.................	Cliff, fishing pole and line
8.................	Hour-glass, snowman, race car set
9.................	Tad-pole, golf club, sperm
10.................	Bat and ball, Laurel and Hardy

Write your "Number-Shape" word next to its corresponding number.

<u>Number</u>   **<u>"Number-Shape" Word</u>**

1.

2.

3.

4.

5.

6.

7.

8.

9.

10.

Now, take some time to vividly picture your "Number-Shaper" images. First think of the number, then picture the image that goes with it. Do this in numerical order (1 - 10). Now try it in reverse numerical order (10 - 1). Try picking numbers at random and see how fast you can visualize each "Number-Shape" image. Now cover the numbers and see if you can remember which number goes with each picture. (The idea is to get the images planted firmly into your memory.)

Draw your "Number-Shape" images in the space below. (You're the only one who'll see these pictures so don't worry about how they look.)

NUMBER   "NUMBER-SHAPE" PICTURE

1.

2.

3.

4.

5.

NUMBER   "NUMBER-SHAPE" PICTURE

6.

7.

8.

9.

10.

Congratulations! You have just learned your first Peg-List. You can use this list over and over again to help you memorize all sorts of things. Let's see how it works as we memorize the item-list below.

Following, is a list of ten items. We will *link* each of these items to our new peg-list. We must link the first item to our first peg, the second item to our second peg and so on.

ITEM LIST

1. **Canoe**
2. **Football**
3. **Hat**
4. **Truck**
5. **Book**

6. **Alarm Clock**
7. **Bowling Ball**
8. **Revenge** (Needs symbolic picture)
9. **Pillow**
10. **Blimp**

(I can't possibly know which "Number-Shape" images you chose, therefore, in the following explanations, I will use my own. If your images are different simply substitute them for the ones I'm using and make up your own link.) Here we go. . .

My first "Number-Shape" peg is *pencil*. The idea is to link "canoe" with *pencil*. Imagine you are paddling down a stream in a giant carved out **pencil** instead of a **canoe**. If your "Number-Shape" image is different, substitute it. (Don't forget to use your memory aids. Smell the smells; feel the feelings; see the colors; and FORM VIVID PICTURES!)

My second "Number-Shape" peg is *swan*. We need to link *swan* to "football." Imagine you are at a **football** game and the players are using a **swan** instead of a football. When the quarter-back passes the swan, it flies away and they have to stop the game.

Breasts to "hat"- picture a nude woman dancing around a room with a giant **hat** covering her **breasts**.

Sailboat to "truck"- picture hundreds of **truck**s floating around in the ocean instead of **sailboat**s. (Make sure you picture these images vividly!)

Fish-hook to "book"- Picture tying a **book** to your fishing line. You are using the book instead of a **hook**. See yourself reeling in a fish that swallowed the book! The fish's stomach has the shape of the book.

Cherry to "alarm clock"- Picture a **cherry** tree that has **alarm clock**s growing off it. You can see George Washington cutting down the tree. With each strike of the axe you can see alarm clocks shaking loose from the branches.

Cliff to "bowling ball"- Picture yourself rolling a gigantic **bowling ball** off a **cliff**. The ball crashes into a house below and crushes it!

Hour-glass to "Rambo"(revenge) See Rambo (**revenge**) firing an explosive arrow into a gigantic crystal **hour-glass**.

He was getting revenge on the hour-glass because it wasn't keeping good time. When it explodes you can see and feel sand flying everywhere.

Golf club to "pillow"- Picture golfers hitting **pillow**s with their **golf club**s instead of golf balls. You can see feathers flying all over the place. The course is covered with feathers.

Bat and ball to "blimp"- You just hit a **ball** with your **bat** and it went so high that it hit a blimp passing overhead. The blimp explodes and tumbles to the ground!

All you need to do to remember the items from the list you just memorized is think of the peg (the "Number-Shape" image); your memory will take care of the rest. The image you created using the peg and the item, will instantly pop into your head. If I wished to remember the second item on the list, I would picture my "Number-Shape" image for the number 2 which is *swan*, and this would remind me of the absurd fantasy I created with swan and **football**! If I wanted to remember the eighth item I would picture *hour-glass* (my "Number-Shape" image for the number 8) and that would remind me of Rambo. Seeing as Rambo is my symbolic picture for **revenge**, I know the eighth item is revenge!

Mentally run through your "Number-Shape" pegs in numerical order and see if you can remember the items you connected to them. If you have any problems, go back and strengthen your associations. Be sure to use your "Memory Aids!"

Exercise

Without looking at the item-list, fill in the items that you linked to your "Number-Shape" peg-list. First, write them down in numerical order in the spaces below. Then, write them in reverse numerical order (without looking at the previous answers) and finally in random numerical order (as depicted below).

1. _____   6. _____
2. _____   7. _____
3. _____   8. _____
4. _____   9. _____
5. _____   10. _____

10. _____   5. _____
9. _____   4. _____
8. _____   3. _____
7. _____   2. _____
6. _____   1. _____

4. _____   5. _____
9. _____   2. _____
8. _____   10. _____
6. _____   1. _____
7. _____   3. _____

You have just memorized a list of ten unrelated items and you know them in and out of order! A person with an untrained memory would find that task *extremely* difficult.

PRACTICE MAKES PERFECT

Make up your own item-list and memorize it using the "Number-Shape" peg-list. (Each time you use the system you will be reinforcing the "Number-Shape" pegs and exercising your creative imagination.) Have a friend make up a list of ten items. (Make sure he writes them down because he'll never remember them.) Have him read the items to you; as he does, link them to your peg-list. Amaze him as you remember all ten items both in and out of order.

NOTE: *You needn't worry about confusing new lists of items with previous lists. You can use the "Number-Shape" system over and over again. Old lists will naturally fade from your memory, unless of course you don't want them to. If you wish to retain a list for a long period of time you must review it. After a few reviews, you will remember the list without having to think of the pegs.*

Suggestions for reviewing

Review the list you wish to remember three times the first day. Each review should be a few hours apart. On the second day review twice about eight hours apart. Then review a couple of days after that, and once more a week later.

NOTE: *These suggestions are not carved in stone. Although this method works well for most people, you should experiment to find what works best for you.*

In the next chapter we will learn another peg system that is based on the numbers 1 - 10. It is called the "Number-Rhyme" system. It can be used in conjunction with the "Number-Shape" system to give you a total of twenty pegs.

CHAPTER 8

THE NUMBER-RHYME SYSTEM

The "Number-Rhyme" system is similar to the "Number-Shape" system. The difference being that for the "Number-Rhyme" system, you will choose an image that *rhymes* with each of the numbers (1 - 10); where as with the "Number-Shape" system, you chose images that had the same *shapes* as the numbers (1 - 10).

Sun *rhymes* with **one**; therefore, we could use *sun* to represent the number 1. For 2 you might choose *shoe* because **shoe** rhymes with **two**.

Following, is a list of suggested "Number-Rhyme" images. Be sure to choose images that are easy for *you* to remember. If you think of an image that you like better than the images I've listed, use it.

NUMBERS	"NUMBER-RHYME" IMAGES
One	Gun, bun, nun, sun,
Two	Shoe, brew (as in beer)
Three	Pea, tree, knee
Four	Door, core (as in apple core), mower

NUMBERS	"NUMBER-RHYME" IMAGES
Five	Hive (as in bee hive), chive
Six	Sticks, bricks
Seven	Heaven
Eight	Gate, date, bait
Nine	Vine, wine, pine (as in pine cone), twine
Ten	Hen, pen (don't use pen if you used it in the "Number-Shape" system)

Write your "Number-Rhyme" word next to its corresponding number.

Number	**"Number-Rhyme" Word**
1.	
2.	
3.	
4.	
5.	
6.	
7.	
8.	
9.	
10.	

Now, take some time to vividly picture the images you chose to represent each number. First, think of the number then picture the image that goes with it. Do this in numerical order (1 - 10). Now try it in reverse numerical order (10 - 1). Try picking numbers at random and see how fast you can visualize the "Number-Rhyme" image. Now cover the numbers and see if you can remember which number goes with each picture. (The idea is to get the images planted firmly into your memory.)

Draw your "Number-Rhyme" images in the spaces below and on the next page.

NUMBER   "NUMBER-RHYME" PICTURE

1.

2.

3.

4.

5.

NUMBER   "NUMBER-RHYME" PICTURE

6.

7.

8.

9.

10.

You will use the "Number-Rhyme" system the same way you used the "Number-Shape" system.

Following, is a list of ten items. We will *link* each of these items to the "Number-Rhyme" peg-list.

ITEM LIST

1. **Arrow**
2. **Typewriter**
3. **Canon**
4. **Couch**
5. **House**
6. **Painting**
7. **Nickel**
8. **Playing Card**
9. **Tennis Match**
10. **Drums**

I don't know which "Number-Rhyme" images you chose, therefore, in the following explanations I will use my own. If your images are different simply substitute them for the ones I'm using and make up your own link.

My first "Number-Rhyme" image is *sun*. We must link "arrow" with *sun*. You look up at the **sun** and see a giant **arrow** sticking out of it.

Shoe to "typewriter"- You are wearing two **typewriters** instead of **shoes**! See yourself walking down the street in these typewriters.

Pea to "canon"- You see a **canon** fire off a **pea** the size of a cannon ball. You watch as it hits a nearby house and splatters green all over it.

Core to "couch"- You are sitting in a **couch** that is carved out of a huge apple **core**! You can feel the apple juice soaking through your clothes.

Hive to "house"- You are living in an enormous bee-**hive** instead of a **house**. The walls are all made of honey-comb.

Sticks to "painting"- You have bunches of **sticks** hanging on your walls instead of **painting**s. Your friends come to your house to admire these works of art.

Heaven to "nickel"- It's raining **nickel**s from **heaven**. You can hear them smashing off the ground.

Pine to "tennis match"- You are watching a **tennis match** being played with a **pine** cone instead of a tennis ball!

Hen to "drum"- Picture a **hen** playing a set of **drums**.

All you need to do to remember the items from the list you just memorized is think of the peg (the "Number-Rhyme" image); your memory will take care of the rest. The image you created using the peg and the item, will instantly pop into your head. If I wished to remember the tenth item on the list, I would picture my "Number-Rhyme" image for the number 10 which is *hen*, and the image of a hen playing a set of drums would come to mind. I would know that the tenth item is drum.

Mentally run through your "Number-Rhyme" pegs in numerical order and see if you can remember the items you connected to them. If you have any problems, go back and strengthen your associations. Be sure to use your "Memory Aids!"

Exercise

Without looking at the item-list, fill in the items that you linked to your "Number-Rhyme" peg-list. First, write them down in numerical order in the spaces below. Then, write them in reverse numerical order (without looking at the previous answers) and finally in random numerical order (as depicted below).

1. _____   6. _____
2. _____   7. _____
3. _____   8. _____
4. _____   9. _____
5. _____   10. _____

10. _____   5. _____
9. _____   4. _____
8. _____   3. _____
7. _____   2. _____
6. _____   1. _____

4. _____   5. _____
9. _____   2. _____
8. _____   10. _____
6. _____   1. _____
7. _____   3. _____

You now have the ability to memorize twenty unrelated items both in and out of order. Let's try it with the following exercise.

Exercise

In combining both "Number-Rhyme" and "Number-Shape" systems, you have the ability to remember a total of twenty items (two sets of ten) in and out of order! I would like you to peg the following list of twenty items to your "Number-Shape" and "Number-Rhyme" peg-lists. Let one of the peg-lists represent the first ten items (numbers 1 - 10) and the other represent the last ten items (numbers 11 - 20). Don't forget to use your memory aids. They are important! Take no more than five minutes to complete the exercise. Start now.

ITEM LIST

1. **Bubble Gum**
2. **Letter**
3. **Charcoal**
4. **Test Tube**
5. **Wig**
6. **Airplane**
7. **Sweetness**
8. **Spoon**
9. **Paper Clip**
10. **Rusty Pipe**

11. **Leaves**
12. **Shopping Cart**
13. **Cassette**
14. **Motor-Cycle**
15. **Rat**
16. **Peace**
17. **Pilgrim**
18. **Rose**
19. **Fire Place**
20. **Jackie Gleason**

Without looking at the item-list, fill in the items that you linked to your "Number-Shape" peg-list. First, write them in numerical order, then write them in reverse numerical order (without looking at the previous answers), and finally in random numerical order (as depicted below).

1. _____	11. _____
2. _____	12. _____
3. _____	13. _____
4. _____	14. _____
5. _____	15. _____
6. _____	16. _____
7. _____	17. _____
8. _____	18. _____
9. _____	19. _____
10. _____	20. _____

20. _____	10. _____
19. _____	9. _____
18. _____	8. _____
17. _____	7. _____
16. _____	6. _____
15. _____	5. _____
14. _____	4. _____
13. _____	3. _____
12. _____	2. _____
11. _____	1. _____

15. _____	11. _____
4. _____	14. _____
9. _____	19. _____
5. _____	18. _____
10. _____	3. _____
12. _____	13. _____
8. _____	17. _____
20. _____	2. _____
1. _____	16. _____
7. _____	6. _____

How did it go? If you had any problems don't get upset, simply review the item list and make stronger associations. Ask yourself, "Did I apply the memory aids? Did I form vivid pictures in my head? Were the associations I created crazy, illogical, absurd, ridiculous, sensuous, or exaggerated? Did I use ACTION in my pictures? Did I take the time to really *learn* the peg images?" If you did then I'm sure you had no problem with the exercise.

We have covered a lot of territory in the last two chapters. You are now familiar with peg lists and how they work. When you are comfortable *using* the "Number-Rhyme" and "Number-Shape" systems, you will be memorizing lists almost as fast as you can read them! The only way to get comfortable with them is to PRACTICE! You should take a day or so to absorb the lists. Review them in your mind whenever you get the chance.

Before continuing on to the next chapter, make up a few lists of your own and apply the peg systems you've learned.

In the chapters ahead, you will be learning how to memorize names and faces, long digit numbers, weekly appointments, speeches, and even BOOKS! You also will learn the "Major" peg-system which will allow you to memorize lists of thousands of items! If you follow me thus far, you're on your way.

CHAPTER 9

THE LOCI SYSTEM

Let's take a trip back in time to the year **500 B.C.**! Imagine that we've just entered the home of a great orator. As we walk from room to room, what do you see? Do you see pencils, pens, notebooks, typewriters or computers? Of course not! They didn't have such handy tools back then. How did the great orators of the time learn a two hour speech? Today we would put it down on paper and study it until we learned it. Back then they had to learn a speech strictly by memory! They accomplished such memory feats by associating each thought of a speech to different *rooms* or *items* in their homes. These were called "Loci." ("Loci," meaning "places," is of Latin origin.) The opening thought of the speech might be associated with the front door; the second thought might be associated with a table in the front hallway; the third thought might be associated with a statue in the front hallway, and so on. These items of course were used sequentially, that is, in the order in which they were encountered upon entering the home. To remember the speech, the orator would take a mental caravan through his home. Thinking of the front door would remind him of the first thought; thinking of the table in the hall-way would remind him of the second thought, and so on. He would continue in this fashion for the rest of the speech.

We automatically assume that pens and pencils have been around since the beginning of time. Obviously they have not. Back then, a good memory was imperative. In fact, it was common for people to walk through a town seeking buildings in which to find new "Loci!"

As you may have surmised, the "Loci" system is nothing more than a *peg-list* consisting of items from your home. It is an easy to use system because you are already intimately familiar with the pegs. Associations that you make with "Loci" pegs will make a greater impression on you because you have a vested interest in them; they belong to *you*. A cow exploding on *your* couch is apt to affect you more, than if the cow blew up on someone else's couch.

Let's build a "Loci" peg-list

Our basic "Loci" peg-list will consist of *twenty* items. We will use five different items in each of four different rooms. Once you really know the system, feel free to expand the list to as many items as you'd like.

First, you must choose four *consecutive* rooms in your house. Each room should lead into the next. For example, when I enter my house through the back door I come into the kitchen; the kitchen is the 1st room on my loci peg-list. My kitchen leads into the dining room; the dining room is the 2nd room on my loci peg-list. When I leave the dining room, I come to the den; the den is the 3rd room. The closest room from the den is my bathroom; I use the bathroom as the 4th room. *Your house most likely has a different layout than mine, so your room list would obviously be different.*

Take out a clean sheet of paper and write down (in order) the first four rooms you would encounter as you walked through your home. (Don't walk around the house to do this; you must picture each room in your mind.)

Now that you have your room list, you need to choose five items from each room. You must work around the room in either a clockwise or counter-clockwise direction and pick out five **large** items. For example; Upon entering my kitchen from my back door, if I were to walk in a counter-clockwise direction, the first large item I would encounter is my oven. The oven is my first peg. The next large item in my kitchen would be the sink; the sink is my second peg. The next item that I come to is the stove; the stove is my third peg, and so on.

There are a few things to keep in mind while choosing your items:

1. Don't use any duplicates. If you are using a **chair** in the dining room, don't use a **chair** in the living room. If you are using a **television** in one room, don't use a **television** in another room etc.

2. You must remember to choose "LARGE" items. (The larger the item, the better.)

3. Be *consistent* in your clockwise or counter-clockwise ordering. In other words, if you work clockwise through the kitchen, work clockwise through the rest of the rooms.

4. Try to leave a little space between the items you choose. It will make your mental picture much clearer.

On the following page, I would like you to write down in sequence, your list of twenty items. Make sure you list them in the order you would encounter them as you walked through your home! (If **couch** is the *first* item in room number *two*, it should be the *sixth* item on your list.) Remember, no walking around the house; use your minds eye. Vividly visualize each item you choose. Do this now.

"LOCI" PEG-LIST

Room 1

1.

2.

3.

4.

5.

Room 2

6.

7.

8.

9.

10.

Room 3

11.

12.

13.

14.

15.

Room 4

16.

17.

18.

19.

20.

I would like you to mentally review your "Loci" peg-list. Picture each item as vividly as you can. After you go through the list from beginning to end, you should go through it again from end to beginning; then review it one more time from beginning to end. (*Do not concern yourself with remembering the number of each item. You don't have to know that "couch" is the 12th item in your list or "table" is the 5th item etc. All you need to know is the **order** in which the items appear.*)

By now you should be fairly comfortable with your "Loci" list. Lets try it out with the following exercise.

Exercise
Below, is a list of twenty items to peg to your "Loci" list. Picture the peg, then picture the item, then link them in a crazy, illogical way. Use color, exaggeration, absurdity, sensuality, quantity etc. See the pictures vividly and in detail. Use all your senses. Spend thirty seconds memorizing each word. Start now!

ITEM LIST

1. **Shoe**	11. **Marshmallow**
2. **Boulder**	12. **Tiger**
3. **Necklace**	13. **Authority**
4. **Tire**	14. **Balloon**
5. **Happiness**	15. **Cannon**
6. **Dump Truck**	16. **Flea Market**
7. **Beethoven**	17. **Lawn Mower**
8. **Space Shuttle**	18. **Saddle**
9. **Cigar**	19. **Orange Juice**
10. **Dental Floss**	20. **Glue**

Without looking at the item list on the previous page, fill in the items that you linked to your "Loci" peg-list.

1. _____
2. _____
3. _____
4. _____
5. _____
6. _____
7. _____
8. _____
9. _____
10. _____
11. _____
12. _____
13. _____
14. _____
15. _____
16. _____
17. _____
18. _____
19. _____
20. _____

If you missed any of the words, it was for one of three reasons. You didn't know your pegs, you didn't form clear pictures using your memory aids, or, you didn't use enough ACTION. If necessary, go back over any word you missed and add the missing ingredient to the image. Now, go through the list again and see if you didn't miss any of them. You probably got them all this time.

As with the "Number-Shape" and the "Number-Rhyme" systems, you can use the "Loci" system to remember "To Do" lists and "Shopping" lists or any list for that matter. The "Loci" system is especially helpful for memorizing speeches, short stories, and jokes.

As I have stated before, feel free to add to the list. You might add more rooms or even more items per room. Also, you don't have to limit your "Loci" to your home. You can use other homes or buildings such as a school or office! You can expand your list to contain hundreds of items. Do as the Romans did; Use your imagination!

CHAPTER 10

NAMES AND PEOPLE

Remembering names is extremely important. When you call someone by their name it makes them feel liked. When you remember a person's name you are putting yourself at an advantage; you are winning that person to your side.

<u>There are three steps to remembering a person's name:</u>

Step 1.

Turn the name into a picture using word substitution. Make sure the picture is either a *sound-alike* or a *symbolic* picture. For example; A sound-alike word for a person named Dominic, is **domino**. Domino works well because you can see a domino and it sounds like Dominic. We could use **hotdog** to *symbolically* represent the name Frank.

NOTE: *Sometimes, when we are introduced to a person we don't actually hear the name. You can't substitute a picture for a name if you don't hear it in the first place. If this should happen, don't be embarrassed to ask for the name to* *be repeated; that person will be flattered to see you are interested enough to ask again.*

Step 2.

Select an outstanding feature or article of clothing on that person. Use the first thing you notice as you will be sure to notice it again! It could be a big nose, long sideburns, a green tie, a polka dot dress, a thick moustache, long earrings, etc. This will act as a peg to which you'll link the person's name.

Step 3.

Link the image that you chose for the persons name to the outstanding feature or article of clothing.

Let's assume you are at a party and you are introduced to the following people. Here's how you'd remember their names:

Example 1: You are introduced to a woman named Ceal and you notice she's wearing big round earrings. All you need to do is turn her name into a picture (using word substitution) and link it to her earrings. You might see hundreds of *seals* jumping through her *earrings*; or you might see *seals* balancing her *earrings* on their noses.

Example 2: You are introduced to a young man named Billy. You notice he is wearing an odd colored tie. Picture a *Billy Goat* chewing on his *tie* and you'll remember his name. The next time you see him you will notice that strange tie he is wearing and the image of a *Billy Goat* chewing on it will pop back into your head. He is in effect wearing his name on his tie!

Example 3: You are introduced to Mr. Marconi. You notice he has big ears. You could picture your **ma** smashing a gigantic ice-cream **cone** into his ear! **Ma cone** (Don't worry about the E sound at the end of Marconi. Your true memory will remember the name is Marconi and not Macone.) You also might have pictured a miniature radio sticking out of Mr. Marconi's ear; or 2 giant ghetto blasters dangling from his ears. This would be a *symbolic* picture linking him to Guglielmo Marconi, the inventor of the radio.

Example 4:   You are introduced to a woman named Mrs. Bagdonovitch. You notice she has big round eyes. You could picture a **witch** with a **bag on** her head. The witch is flying out of her eye on a broom; **bag on a witch!** *With a little imagination, you can remember any name!*

If you wish to remember a person's name and occupation, turn each into a picture then use them both in the same crazy image. For example; You've just met Doug Ashby and he sells shoes. You notice that Doug has a large nose. You could picture a **shoe** sticking out of his nose with a miniature **dog** (Doug) sitting on the end of it smoking a cigarette. The dog is flipping the **ash**es from the cigarette at a giant **bee** that is swarming around him (**ash bee**).

NOTE: *It took a lot of words for me to describe this scene to you but it only takes a second to picture in your mind!*

Once you have linked a person's name to a peg on his body, you should review that image a few times within the first five minutes. With each review, you should picture the image as vividly as possible. This will help lock it into your memory.

If you know you will be seeing a person again at a later date, don't use an article of clothing as your peg. He or she will most likely be wearing different clothes the next time you meet. Instead, peg the person's name to a facial feature.

In picking out a peg on a person's face, you should choose something unique, something that you'll be sure to recognize the next time you meet. Every face is different so this shouldn't be too difficult. With a little practice you will spot unique features quickly. Start studying the faces you see on TV; that's a good way to learn. You might spend a couple of days studying lips and a couple of days studying noses then a couple of days analyzing eyebrows etc. (See "Head and Facial Features" below.) *Normally when we look at a person's face we see it as a whole. We do not analyze each part of it in detail. Consequently, we are not truly aware of the subtle differences that exist between faces. As you study them a little closer these differences will become more apparent.*

Head and Facial Features

As you look at a face, ask yourself the following questions:

1. Is the overall shape of the head large, medium, or small?

2. Is the face round, triangular, square, rectangular, or oval?

3. Is the hair thick, fine, bald, receding, parted, wavy, straight, frizzy, or cropped?

4. Is the forehead wide, narrow, high, smooth, or lined? How much space is there between the hair line and the eyebrows or between each temple?

5. Are the eyelashes thick, thin, long, short, straight, or curled?

6. Are the eyebrows long, short, bushy, or thin? Do they meet in the middle or are they spaced apart? Are they flat, winged, arched, or tapered?

7. Are the eyes small, large, protruding, deep-seated, close together, spaced apart, slanted outward or inward, or colored? What color are they?

8. Is the nose straight, flat, pointed, pug, large, medium, small, narrow, or wide? Are the nostrils hairy?

9. Are the cheekbones high or hidden?

10. Are the ears large, small, round, oblong, flat against the head, protruding from the head, large-lobed, or no lobe?

11. Are the lips small, large, up-turned, down-turned, well shaped, or slanted? Is the upper lip long or short?

12. Is the chin square, pointed, round, double, dimpled, protruding, or receding?

13. Is the skin dark, light, blemished, rough, smooth, oily, dry, or wrinkled?

Name Picture Vocabulary

Once you use a picture for a name, you will find yourself using the same picture for other people with the same name. For example, my picture for the name Ed is *horse*. I use "Mr.

Ed" (a horse) to symbolically represent the name ED. Whenever I meet someone named Ed I automatically picture a "horse" and link it to a peg on that person. I use horse for every Ed I meet, it's a standard. For Tony I use *tiger*, "Tony the Tiger." Whenever I meet someone named Tony, the picture of a tiger instantly comes to mind.

I have standard pictures for almost five hundred first names. The benefits to having a "Picture Vocabulary" are obvious. I needn't spend valuable time doing word substitutions on the spot. It pays off when I meet a group of people in rapid succession! You will begin to form your own "standard" name pictures as you continue using the memory techniques.

For your convenience, I have listed a few hundred of the most common first names in America. Next to the name is a space to write your picture-word for it. In choosing your picture word, use the principles discussed in this chapter and in the chapter on Word Substitution. Once you have filled in words for all the names, you'll find you already know most of them by memory!

Helpful Hints: Use the first appropriate picture that pops into your head. It will likely be the first thing to pop into your head the next time you see or hear the name. It might be a symbolic picture or a sound-alike picture. If you have a friend or relative named Sue, use her as your picture for the name Sue. When you meet someone named Sue, associate your friend or relative to the peg you choose on that person. The same thing goes for Famous people. You might use Ronald McDonald or Ronald Reagan to represent the name Ronald. You could use the Presidential Seal to represent Ronald. The point is, use pictures that you'll remember easily.

Female Names

Abby _____

Abigail _____

Ada _____

Adelle _____

Adora _____

Adrian _____

Agatha _____

Agnes _____

Aileen _____

Alberta _____

Alexandra _____

Alexis _____

Alice _____

Alison _____

Alixe _____

Alyssa _____

Amanda _____

Ambrose _____

Amelia _____

Amy _____

Andrea _____

Angela _____

Angelica _____

Angie _____

Anita _____

Ann _____

Anna _____

Annette _____

Antoinette _____

April _____

Arlene _____

Audrey _____

Ava _____

Barbara _____

Becky _____

Belinda _____

Bernadette _____

Bernadine _____

Bernice _____

Beth _____

Betty _____

Bev _____

Beverly _____

Bobbi _____

Brenda _____

Bridget _____

Camille _____

Candace _____

Carla _____

Carlotta _____

Carol _____

Catherine _____

Ceal   _____

Cecillia   _____

Charlene   _____

Charlotte   _____

Charmaine   _____

Chris   _____

Christina   _____

Cindy   _____

Claire   _____

Claudia   _____

Collen   _____

Connie   _____

Cynthia   _____

Daisy   _____

Darlene   _____

Dawn   _____

Debbie   _____

Denise   _____

Desiree   _____

Diane   _____

Dianna   _____

Dina   _____

Dolores   _____

Donna   _____

Doris   _____

Dorothy   _____

Dottie   _____

Edith   _____

Edna   _____

Eileen   _____

Elaine   _____

Eleanor   _____

Elena   _____

Elizabeth   _____

Ellen   _____

Erica   _____

Eva   _____

Evalyn   _____

Faith   _____

Flora   _____

Frances   _____

Georgia   _____

Ginny   _____

Gloria   _____

Grace   _____

Harriett   _____

Heather   _____

Helen   _____

Helena   _____

Hope   _____

Ida   _____

Irene   _____

Jacqueline   _____

Jane   _____

Janet _____

Jean _____

Jenniffer _____

Jessica _____

Jill _____

Joan _____

Joanna _____

Jocelyn _____

Josephine _____

Joy _____

Joyce _____

Juanita _____

Judy _____

Julia _____

Julie _____

Juliet _____

June _____

Justine _____

Kara _____

Karen _____

Kate _____

Kathleen _____

Kathy _____

Kay _____

Kitty _____

Krista _____

Kristin _____

Laura   _____

Leslie   _____

Lillian   _____

Linda   _____

Lisa   _____

Lois   _____

Lora   _____

Lorrain   _____

Lucy   _____

Luisa   _____

Lynn   _____

Madonna   _____

Maggie   _____

Marcie   _____

Margaret   _____

Marge   _____

Margy   _____

Maria   _____

Marian   _____

Marilyn   _____

Marsha   _____

Mary   _____

Maureen   _____

Maxine   _____

Melanie   _____

Melissa   _____

Michelle   _____

Millie   _____

Mimi   _____

Molly   _____

Nancy   _____

Natalie   _____

Nelly   _____

Netta   _____

Nina   _____

Nita   _____

Nora   _____

Pam   _____

Pat   _____

Patricia   _____

Patty   _____

Paula   _____

Pauline   _____

Peg   _____

Peggy   _____

Phyllis   _____

Polly   _____

Rachel   _____

Regina   _____

Rita   _____

Roberta   _____

Ronnie   _____

Rosa   _____

Rosalie   _____

Rose   _____

Rosemary   _____

Rosie   _____

Ruth   _____

Sally   _____

Sandra   _____

Sandy   _____

Sara   _____

Sharon   _____

Sheila   _____

Silvia   _____

Sonia   _____

Stella   _____

Stephanie   _____

Sue   _____

Susan   _____

Susanna   _____

Suzie   _____

Terri   _____

Theresa   _____

Tina   _____

Toni   _____

Valerie   _____

Vanessa   _____

Vera   _____

Veronica   _____

Vicky   _____

Victoria _____
Virginia _____
Wanda _____
Wendy _____
Yvonne _____

Male Names

Aaron _____
Abott _____
Abdul _____
Adam _____
Al _____
Alan _____
Albert _____
Alec _____
Alex _____
Alexander _____
Alfred _____
Alphonse _____
Andrew _____
Andy _____
Anthony _____
Arnold _____
Art _____
Artie _____
Barry _____
Ben _____

Bill   _____

Billy   _____

Bob   _____

Bobby   _____

Brandan   _____

Brian   _____

Bruce   _____

Bud   _____

Buddy   _____

Burt   _____

Carl   _____

Chad   _____

Dharles   _____

Chris   _____

Christopher _____

Chuck   _____

Clark   _____

Colin   _____

Dan   _____

Daniel   _____

Danny   _____

Dave   _____

David   _____

Dennis   _____

Dominic   _____

Don   _____

Donald   _____

Doug   _____

Ed   _____

Eric   _____

Eugene   _____

Fran   _____

Francis   _____

Frank   _____

Franny   _____

Fred   _____

Gavin   _____

Gene   _____

George   _____

Gerald   _____

Greg   _____

Gregory   _____

Hank   _____

Harold   _____

Harry   _____

Henry   _____

Jack   _____

Jacob   _____

James   _____

Jamie   _____

Jared   _____

Jason   _____

Jeff   _____

Jeffrey   _____

Jerry _____

Jim _____

Joesph _____

John _____

Justin _____

Ken _____

Kenneth _____

Kevin _____

Kieth _____

Larry _____

Leo _____

Linus _____

Lou _____

Luke _____

Mark _____

Martin _____

Matt _____

Matthew _____

Max _____

Michael _____

Mike _____

Nathan _____

Nicholas _____

Nick _____

Oscar _____

Pat _____

Patrick _____

Paul　　　　_____

Pete　　　　_____

Peter　　　　_____

Phil　　　　_____

Philip　　　　_____

Quincy　　　　_____

Ralph　　　　_____

Randy　　　　_____

Ray　　　　_____

Raymond　　　_____

Rich　　　　_____

Richard　　　_____

Rick　　　　_____

Rob　　　　_____

Robert　　　_____

Roger　　　_____

Ron　　　　_____

Ronald　　　_____

Roy　　　　_____

Salvatore　　_____

Sam　　　　_____

Sean　　　　_____

Sidney　　　_____

Silvester　　_____

Simon　　　_____

Stan　　　　_____

Stanley　　　_____

Stephen   _____

Steve   _____

Ted   _____

Teddy   _____

Theo   _____

Theodore   _____

Thomas   _____

Tim   _____

Timmy   _____

Timothy   _____

Toby   _____

Tom   _____

Tommy   _____

Tony   _____

Vance   _____

Vick   _____

Victor   _____

Walt   _____

Walter   _____

Will   _____

William   _____

Willy   _____

Zachary   _____

Exercise

Use the name list to test yourself; First cover the names and try to remember them from the picture-words. Then reverse it; cover the picture-words and try to remember them by looking at the names. You'll be amazed at how quickly you can learn them. (You'll have a tremendous edge if you take the time to commit them to memory.)

Start applying the memory techniques for remembering names and people, right away. Use them whenever you meet someone new.

CHAPTER 11

THE PHONETIC ALPHABET SYSTEM

Numbers are intangible objects. They are nothing more than two dimensional drawings. They are normally very difficult to remember, but, The "Phonetic-Alphabet" system will change all that.

The system you are about to learn is the most powerful memory system of all. It will enable you to remember phone numbers, dates, prices, credit-card numbers, license numbers, formulas, equations, statistics, numbers and lists of any length! It has been around for over three-hundred years. This system breaks all boundaries of previous, more limited systems. It is in itself, limitless. Best of all, it is easy to learn.

The "Phonetic-Alphabet" system will enable us to build words that represent numbers. This is done with a special code consisting of ten digits, 0 thru 9; and ten consonant *sounds*. Each of the digits (0 - 9) is paired with a consonant *sound*.

We will need to memorize the consonant *sound* that represents each of the ten digits. Once that is done, we can build words with those sounds. We can then use our memory techniques to memorize the words. Those words can later be recalled and translated back into numbers. I will show you the process step-by-step but first let's look at the following code:

"Phonetic-Alphabet" Code

0 = s, z, soft c
1 = t,d
2 = n
3 = m
4 = r
5 = l
6 = j, sh, ch, dg, soft g
7 = k, hard c, hard g, q
8 = f, v
9 = b, p

Keep in mind, it is the **sounds** we are looking for not the spelling! Let's take a closer look at the consonants.

The digit "0" is represented by the sound of the consonants s, z, and soft c. Say the following words out loud: *keys, zero, shoelace.* Did you notice how each of the consonant sounds were very similar? Say them again and notice how your tongue, teeth, and lips form the same shape when you pronounce these consonants. *Memory aid:* To remember the consonant sound for the digit 0 simply pronounce the word *zero.* That's easy enough!

The digit "1" is represented by the sound of the consonants t and d. Say the following words out loud: *tape, wind, hot, dip.* Did you notice the similarities between the d and t consonant sounds? Say them again and notice how your tongue, teeth, and lips form the same shape when you pronounce them. (**NOTE:** *"th" also can be used to repre-*

sent the number 1.) *Memory aid:* To memorize the consonant sound for the number 1 simply remember a typewritten "t" has *one* downstroke. You know how "t" sounds. Take a moment to think about that.

The digit "2" is represented by the sound of the consonant n. To remember the consonant sound for the number 2 simply remember typewritten "n" has *two* down strokes.

The digit "3" is represented by the sound of the consonant m. To remember the consonant sound for the number 3 simply remember typewritten "m" has *three* down strokes.

The digit "4" is represented by the sound of the consonant r. To remember the consonant sound for the number 4 simply remember "r" is the last letter in the word fou**r**.

The digit "5" is represented by the sound of the consonant L. I would like you to hold your left hand in front of you with the back of your hand facing you. Now spread your **5** fingers out as far as you can. Notice how your forefinger and thumb form the shape of an L. L = 5 and 5 = L. It does now and it always will.

The digit "6" is represented by the sound of the consonants j, sh, ch, dg, and soft g. Say the following words out loud: *juice, shoe, cheer, dodge, geography*. Did you notice the similarities between the consonant sounds? Say them again and notice how your tongue, teeth, and lips form the same shape when you pronounce them. You may have noticed that the second "g" in geography was not typed in bold; that was done for a reason. Say the word again slowly and notice the difference between the way the first "g" sounds and the second "g" sounds. The second "g" is a *hard* g not a soft g. Your teeth, lips, and tongue take on a different shape for each. We are interested in the sound of soft g as in *George, cage, germ* etc. The consonants j, sh, ch, dg, and **soft g** all sound alike. Hard g as in *game, ghost,* and *sing* does not sound that way therefore it does not represent the number 6. To memorize the consonant sound for the number 6 simply remember that 6 and J are almost mirror images:

6J

The digit "7" is represented by the sound of the consonants k, hard c, hard g, and q. Say the following words out loud: *book, harmonica, grape, unique*. If you look at the letter K you can see that it looks like it's composed of two 7's with one of the 7's tilted on its side. This is how you remember 7 goes with the sound of the letter K.

K

The digit "8" is represented by the sound of the consonants f and v. Say the following words out loud; *knife, hive*. Again, notice the similarities in sound and mouth position. Notice how your tongue, teeth, and lips form the same shape when you pronounce them. The letter f when written looks like an eight. This is how you remember that "f" goes with the number 8.

ƒ

The digit "9" is represented by the sound of the consonants p and b. Say the following words out loud: *pie, bye, plum, bum*. The number 9 looks like a mirror image of the letter P. This is how you remember that the sound of P goes with 9.

P9

We will use the above consonant sounds in conjunction with the letters a, e, i, o, u, w, h, and y, to build words. Before we try it, look over the "Phonetic-Alphabet" rules on the next page.

"Phonetic-Alphabet" rules:

1. The vowels, a, e, i, o, and u have no numerical value.

2. The letters w, h, and y have no numerical value.

3. Silent letters have no value. For example; the second b in *bomb* is silent therefore it is disregarded.

4. Double letters that produce the same sound count only once. For example; the word *matter* has two t's in it. When the word is pronounced, you only hear one t. On the other hand, the word accident has two c's but each c is pronounced differently. The first is a hard c and the latter a soft c. Hard c translates to 7 and soft c translates to 0. Remember it's the sounds we're interested in not the letters.

5. The letter x transposes according to the way it sounds in a word. For example; in the word *tax,* the t is transposed to 1 and the x transposes to 70. This is because the letter x sounds like **ks**. In the word complexion the x transposes to 76. That is because the x sounds like **ksh**. Say the words out loud to see what I mean.

To make it all clear, let's use a couple of examples. Let's consider the word *bitter*. Say it out loud, bi ter. Aside from the vowels i and e (which don't count) all you hear is the letter b, the letter t, and the letter r. The word bitter then would translate to 914.

In the word *limb*, all that count are the letters l and m. The b is silent and silent letters don't count. The i is a vowel and vowels don't count. Limb then transposes to 53.

In the word *vixen*, the v translates to 8. The x sounds like k and s combined (say it slowly) and therefore translates to 70. The n translates to 2. If we put it all together we get the number 8702.

In the word *election*, the l transposes to 5. The c transposes to 7. The t does **not** transpose to 1 as it usually would. It translates to 6 because it sounds like sh. Finally, the n transposes to 2. If we put it all together we get the number 5762.

At this point I would like you to take some time and thoroughly learn the "Phonetic-Alphabet." Know it to the point that when you see 2 you automatically think n. When you see 4 you immediately think r, and so on. Take some time to absorb it before continuing.

Exercise

Translate the following words and phrases into long-digit numbers. Write them down on a separate piece of paper. When you are through, check them against the answers on the next page.

1. rendezvous
2. hillside
3. pocket
4. lunch
5. tangerine
6. pedal
7. child
8. exaggeration
9. chile
10. Mary had a little lamb
11. cheese and crackers
12. what a beautiful world we live in
13. masque
14. extravagant
15. malign

Answers for previous exercise:

1. 4218
2. 501
3. 971
4. 526
5. 12642
6. 915
7. 651
8. 706462
9. 65
10. 34151553
11. 602174740
12. 19185451582
13. 307
14. 70148721
15. 352

By now you are probably beginning to see just how powerful this system is. You may already have some ideas on what you would like to do with it. In the chapters ahead we will learn some fantastic ways to apply it, but, before we learn to run we must learn to walk. Let's practice turning numbers into words.

Numbers to Words

Turning numbers into words is fairly simple, and it's fun. To do it, you must translate each digit of the number into a letter using the "Phonetic-Alphabet," e.g., 41 = **r t**. Once the number is translated into letters, you build words using a, e, i, o, u, w, h, and y as "wild letters," e.g., **rat, root, art, wart, heart, rate** etc. **NOTE:** *In this example we could have used* *r d instead of r t because 1 translates to either t or d. Other choices might have been; rod, hard, heard etc.*

The principles are the same with large numbers. We must first break a large number down into groups of numbers, then make a word for each group. Groups can be any size, for example; 839562738450 could be broken down into (83 **foam** - 95627 **belching** - 38 movie - 450 **rolls**) *or maybe* (8395 **fumble** - 627 **chunk** - 384 **mover** - 50 **laws**) etc. The way you break a large number down is entirely up to you. Once the number is translated into words you simply connect them using the link system. Let's do that using *foam, belching, movie,* and *rolls*. We will first link **foam** to **belching**; Imagine a giant piece of *foam belching*! (See it vividly in your minds eye.) Now we need to link **belching** to **movie**; Imagine you're sitting in a theater watching a *movie* and everyone is *belching* loudly. Next we link **movie** to **rolls**; Imagine you're watching a home *movie* that is being projected onto the side of a giant white *Rolls* Royce.

The four word link we have just formed holds the key to our 12-digit number. If you know the link you know the number! All we need to do is think of the first word in the link, *foam*, and translate it back into digits; We get 83. Now what does foam remind you of? *Belching* of coarse, and belching translates to 95627. Belching should then remind you of *movie* which translates to 38. And finally, movie reminds you of *Rolls* Royce which translates to 450. Put it all together and you get 839562738450!

Try it on your own this time. Take out a piece of paper and write the numbers down as you go through the link in your mind. If you know the link and you know the sounds you should have no problem. Do it now.

At first, translating might take a little time. But with a little practice you will be translating almost as fast as you can think the word or see the number!

Exercise

Translate the following numbers into words, then link the words. (Try to make words that form images. Remember, we think and link in pictures.) Take out a sheet of paper and without looking at the book write down the numbers. Do them one at a time.

1.) 950113163740
2.) 54729012380378056273
3.) 315625321208840451
4.) 33417270484215621995
5.) 45510162715991011427
6.) 470602795014715

Could you imagine trying to remember those numbers without the system? Do you realize how long it would take you? You may be thinking that you'll never need to remember a 25-digit number, and you probably won't. But think about it, if you can memorize a 25-digit number with ease, imagine the ease with which you'll remember a telephone number!

If at this point you are not *totally* comfortable with the "Phonetic-Alphabet," you should take some time to learn it well! Take out your dictionary and practice changing words into numbers. Anytime you see a number, transpose it in your head. When you're driving, look at license plates and transpose them. (For now, skip the letters on the plate; we'll learn to deal with them a little later.) The point is, do it whenever you can!

This system is the basis for several other systems we will be learning. Learn it *thoroughly* before reading on.

CHAPTER **12**

NUMBERS AND PRICES

You are now equipped with the tools to remember telephone numbers, code numbers, ID numbers, prices, and so on. In the examples below you will see how to apply them.

Telephone Numbers

There are two steps to remembering a telephone number:

1. Translate the number into words using the phonetic alphabet system.
2. Link the words to whomever the number belongs.

Keep in mind, when you translate a number into words, choose words that elicit pictures. We want to avoid using abstracts as they are difficult to remember and our purpose is to make remembering easy. Also, when you form a link, use your memory aids to make it a memorable one.

Ok, let's assume we wish to remember the telephone number for our local post office. We'll assume the number is 977-4740. The first step is to translate it into words using the phonetic alphabet system. We might come up with **bag** and **crackers**. Now all we need to do is link **bag** and **crackers** to post office in a memorable way. Imagine yourself at the **post office** with a gigantic shopping **bag** full of **crackers** and you're telling the clerk you wish to mail them! See yourself taking each cracker out of the bag and placing a stamp on it.

Our work is done. Whenever we wish to remember the telephone number we simply think of post office and the silly image we created with a **bag** of **crackers** will immediately come to mind. All that's left to do is translate **bag** and **crackers** back into numbers and dial away!

If you needed to remember an area code with the number you would simply translate it and include it in your link.

NOTE: *When you translate a telephone number you don't have to conform to the original grouping of the number; e.g., ***-****. In the example above, we broke the number down as 97 - 74740.*

Exercise

Memorize the following phone numbers and link them to the people they belong to. Take no more than five minutes to do so.

1. Dentist   363-1947
2. Butcher   841-3788
3. Fire Station   464-7551
4. Book Store   249-3198

Fill in the correct telephone numbers in the spaces below.

1. Fire Station _____
2. Dentist _____
3. Book Store _____
4. Butcher _____

Code numbers & ID numbers

Remember code numbers and ID numbers the same way as you remembered the telephone number in the previous example. Let's assume that 77394 was the code number to disengage an alarm system in your home. To remember it you'd simply translate 77394 into a word or words and link them to the alarm. It so happens that 77394 translates to **cucumber.** You might see yourself using a tiny cucumber to punch in the code on the key pad of the alarm system, or, you might see a giant cucumber with arms punching in the code for you. It really is easy. Now, whenever you wish to remember the code, simply recall your link and key word(s), and translate them back into numbers.

Prices

Prices are just as easy to remember as any other numbers. The only difference being with prices we must remember the decimal point. Simply link the translated price to whatever item it belongs to. When translating the image back to a number, place the decimal point two numbers in from the right. Let's translate the prices on the following page and link them to their items.

Picture Frame $7.59
Television $471.99
Chain-Saw $96.49

Vividly visualize each of the following descriptions.

The price of the picture frame can be translated into *club* 759. See yourself smashing a **picture frame** with a big **club**! The price of the television can be translated into *rocket, pipe* 47199. You are watching television and someone is building a **rocket** out of a huge **pipe**. The rocket takes off and flies right out of the **television** set and into your living room! (It took 32 words to describe that scene but it only takes a split second to see it!)

The price of the chain-saw can be translated into *pitch, rope* 9649. You see a man **pitch** a **rope** to another man who is holding a **chain-saw**. He swings the chain-saw at the rope and cuts it in half.

Now, when you think picture frame, you'll see yourself smashing it with a **club**. You'll know the price is $7.59. When you think Television, you'll remember the person building a **rocket** out of a huge **pipe**. You'll know the price of the set is $471.99. What was the price of the chain saw? If you took the time to picture the image I described above, you should have no problem remembering a man **pitch**ing a **rope** to another man who was holding the chain-saw. You would know the price is $96.49.

Exercise

Memorize the items and prices on the following page. Take no more than five minutes to do so.

1. Lamp $49.95
2. Hair Dryer $23.89
3. Tool Chest $129.98
4. Yarn $1.75

Without looking at the list above, fill in the correct prices for each item.

1. Hair Dryer   _____
2. Yarn   _____
3. Tool Chest   _____
4. Lamp   _____

Exercise

If you don't know them already, memorize your credit card numbers and license number. Practice recalling them over the next few days in order to lock them in and make them knowledge. You will see that after a while you won't need the silly associations to remember them. After all, that's what memory techniques are all about, they're a means to an end.

CHAPTER 13

THE MAJOR SYSTEM

In learning the "Phonetic-Alphabet" system you have acquired the tools to build a peg-list that has no boundaries! With it you can memorize (in and out of order) anything you'd like. In previous chapters we learned the Number-Shape and Number-Rhyme systems. Both systems allow us to remember lists in and out of order but they are limited to just 10 pegs each. The "Major" peg-list can consist of hundreds or thousands of pegs. There really is no limit!

Take a look at the following list of *pegs*:

"MAJOR" PEGS FOR THE NUMBERS 1-10
1. tie
2. Noah   (picture a gray beard)
3. ma
4. rye
5. law   (use a symbolic picture e.g., police officer)
6. shoe
7. key
8. foe   (picture the face of an enemy)
9. pie
10. toes

If you look closely you will see that each of the pegs in the previous list was built using the "Phonetic-Alphabet" system. The first peg, *tie*, was built using the consonant sound associated with the number 1, which is **t**. "**T**" is the only consonant sound in the word, therefore, tie can only represent the number 1. We could have used other words to represent 1; e.g., **d**ye, ha**t**, **t**ea and so on, but tie seems to work well for most people because it begins with the letter t and it's easy to picture.

Noah contains only one consonant sound, **n**. "**N**" represents the number 2 in the "Phonetic-Alphabet" system, therefore, Noah represents the number 2. (Use the picture of a gray beard to symbolically represent Noah.)

Toes, is the tenth peg in the "Major" system peg-list. Notice it contains two consonant sounds, **t** and **s**. In our "Phonetic-Alphabet," **t** stands for 1 and **s** stands for 0. Put them together and you get the number 10.

I would like you to take some time to learn the first ten pegs of the "Major" system. You are free to use my peg-words or make up your own. If you choose to make up your own words, make sure they form pictures. As you learn them, visualize each picture as vividly as possible. Once a word is chosen to represent a number, don't change it. You want to avoid confusing other word-images for that number. When you have learned the pegs, complete the exercise below.

Exercise

We will link the list of items on the following page to the "Major" pegs. Make sure you form vivid pictures!

ITEM LIST

1. Book
2. Pill
3. Couch
4. Lawn
5. Trumpet
6. Tape
7. Spoon
8. Surf-Board
9. Frisbee
10. Thimble

The first item in the list is *book* and the "Major" peg-word for "1" is *tie*. We must link **book** to **tie**. Picture yourself wearing a long **book** instead of a **tie**.

The second item is *pill* and the "Major" peg-word for 2 is *Noah*. (We will use a gray beard to represent Noah.) Picture a giant **pill** that has a long gray beard (**Noah**).

Couch to *ma* - Picture your **ma** carrying a huge **couch** above her head! (See the picture clearly.)

Lawn to *rye* - Picture thousands of slices of **rye** bread all over your front **lawn**.

Trumpet to *law* - Picture a police officer (**law**) blowing a **trumpet** instead of a whistle. He is directing traffic with a trumpet!

Tape to *shoe* - Imagine that you wrap your feet in Scotch-**tape** instead of putting on **shoe**s! You are walking around in Scotch-tape!

Spoon to *key* - You are trying to open your door with a tiny **spoon** instead of a **key**.

Surf-board to *foe* - Picture yourself using an enemy (**foe**) as a **surf-board**. You are riding the waves as you stand on your enemy.

Frisbee to *pie* - You are using a freshly baked **pie** to play **frisbee**!

Thimble to *toes* - You have **thimbles** on your **toes**. See yourself using your feet to sew!

Now, if you wished to remember what the second item in the list was, you would think 2 and that would give you Noah. Noah will trigger the image of a giant **pill** that has a long **gray beard** (Noah). You will know that the second item is *pill*.

Without looking at the item-list, fill in the items that you linked to your "Major" peg-list. First, write them in numerical order in the spaces below. Then write them in reverse numerical order (without looking at the previous answers) and finally in random numerical order (as depicted on the next page).

1. _____   6. _____
2. _____   7. _____
3. _____   8. _____
4. _____   9. _____
5. _____   10. _____

10. _____   5. _____
9. _____   4. _____
8. _____   4. _____
7. _____   3. _____
6. _____   1. _____

4. _____	5. _____
9. _____	2. _____
8. _____	10. _____
6. _____	1. _____
7. _____	3. _____

In time, you will not have to think of the "Phonetic-Alphabet" to remember your peg words. When you hear or see a number you will automatically think of the peg.

Before continuing, take some time to absorb the first ten "Major" pegs. Make up your own item list and memorize it using the "Major" system.

Below, I have listed peg-words for each number from 11-100. If you know the "Phonetic Alphabet" system well, they should be easy to learn.

As you will see, having standard translations for all one and two digit numbers will be extremely useful! In fact, they will be used extensively in memorizing times and dates. Feel free to use your own words if they work better for you.

"MAJOR" PEGS FOR THE NUMBERS 11-100:

11. tot	21. net	31. mat
12. tin	22. nun	32. moon
13. tomb	23. name	33. mummy
14. tire	24. Nero	34. mower
15. towel	25. nail	35. mule
16. dish	26. notch	36. match
17. dog	27. neck	37. mug
18. dove	28. knife	38. movie
19. tape	29. knob	39. mop
20. nose	30. mouse	40. rose

41. rat	51. lad	61. sheet
42. rain	52. lawn	62. chin
43. ram	53. lime	63. chum
44. rear	54. lure	64. chair
45. roll	55. lily	65. jail
46. roach	56. leech	66. choo-choo
47. rock	57. lock	67. chalk
48. roof	58. lava	68. chef
49. rope	59. lip	69. ship
50. lace	60. cheese	70. case
71. cat	81. fat	91. bat
72. can	82. fan	92. bone
73. comb	83. foam	93. bum
74. car	84. fur	94. bear
75. coal	85. file	95. bell
76. couch	86. fish	96. beach
77. cake	87. fog	97. book
78. cave	88. fife	98. puff
79. cob	89. vibe	99. pipe
80. fuse	90. bus	100. disease

WEEKLY APPOINTMENTS & SCHEDULES

This system uses the Major System to help you remember weekly appointments and schedules. You must know the peg words for the numbers 1 through 80 in order to use it.

There are seven days in a week, therefore, we will assign each day a number (from 1 - 7) beginning with Monday.

1 = Monday
2 = Tuesday
3 = Wednesday
4 = Thursday
5 = Friday
6 = Saturday
7 = Sunday

All we need to do is form a two digit number to represent a day and a time. The first digit will give us the day and the second digit will give us the time. Example; the number 72 represents Sunday at 2:00 because the 7 represents Sunday and the 2 represents 2:00. We can represent Monday at 4:00

with the number 14. The 1 stands for the day, Monday, and the 4 stands for 4 o'clock. The number 24 would translate to Tuesday at 4:00. What number would represent 3:00 on Friday? If you said 53 you are correct, because 5 stands for the fifth day of the week (Friday) and 3 stands for 3:00. It's simple. (*I will show you how to handle 10:00, 11:00, and 12:00 in just a bit.*)

Suppose you wanted to remember your dentist appointment is for Thursday at 9:00. Thursday at 9:00 transposes to 49. As you know, the peg word for 49 is **rope**. All you need to do is link **rope** with **dentist** and you'll remember the appointment. Get a vivid picture of your dentist trying to pull your tooth with a long rope!

Now, suppose you wanted to remember a staff meeting that is scheduled for Tuesday at 2:00. All you have to do is transpose Tuesday at 2:00 and you'll get 22. The peg word for 22 is **nun**. If you link **nun** to **staff meeting** you'll remember it! Imagine yourself sitting in the meeting and all your co-workers are dressed as nuns!

In most cases, you won't need to specify A.M. or P.M. in your little fantasies. The context of the appointment will clue you. For example, you are not likely to attend a staff meeting at 2:00 A.M. nor are you likely to have dental work done at 9:00 P.M.. But, for such cases where you do need to specify A.M. or P.M. there is a simple solution. Simply include the color white in your fantasy if it's A.M. and black if it's P.M.. Therefore, if for some strange reason the dentist appointment was at 9:00 **P.M.**, you could picture the dentist pulling your tooth with a **black** rope.

Now that we know how to deal with days and hours, let's learn how to deal with minutes.

To simplify matters we will deal with quarter hours only; e.g., —:15, —:30, and —:45. If you have an appointment at 9:20, simply remember it as 9:15. (It can't hurt to be five minutes early.) A quarter after the hour will be represented by a **25-cent piece**, half past the hour by a **half grapefruit**, and three-quarters past the hour by **three quarters of a pie**. Let's suppose our staff meeting was Tuesday at 2:30. Picture your co-workers dressed up as nuns and each is eating a giant half grapefruit. All we have done is included the appropriate picture for the quarter hour into our fantasy, in this case it was a half grapefruit. Had the meeting been at 2:15 you would have used 25-cent piece instead of half grapefruit.

For those of you who need to remember the exact minute, use the system (for days and hours) as we have above and deal with minutes by translating them separately. Once they are translated you should put the "minute-image" into a bottle. Let me explain: Assume you have an appointment at 5:41 on Friday. The day and the hour translate to 55 or **lily**. The minutes, 41, translate to **rat**. Your fantasy will now include a picture of your **appointment**, a picture of a **lily** and a picture of a **rat in a bottle**. You must put the picture of minutes into a bottle to prevent it from being confused with the day and the hour. You'll know that the image in the bottle represents minutes. If you don't put them into a bottle, what's to stop you from thinking **rat** stands for Thursday at 1 and lily stands for 55 minutes?

The last thing we need to cover is how to deal with 10:00, 11:00, and 12:00. Let's deal with 10:00 first: Normally Monday at 10:00 would translate to 110. We don't need to use the number 10 to represent 10:00, we can simply let 0 represent it. Therefore, Monday at 10:00 will translate to 10. (The 1 stands for Monday and the 0 stands for 10:00). Our peg word for ten is **toes**. Tuesday at 10:00 would normally be 210 but not if we let 0 represent 10. We can translate Tuesday at 10:00 into 20. Our peg word for 20 is **nose**. I have listed all of the translations for 10:00 on the following page.

Monday at 10:00 = **toes**
Tuesday at 10:00 = **nose**
Wednesday at 10:00 = **mouse**
Thursday at 10:00 = **rose**
Friday at 10:00 = **lace**
Saturday at 10:00 = **cheese**
Sunday at 10:00 = **case**

For 11:00 and 12:00 of each day, we *must* use a three digit number. We need to create a word for each of these three digit numbers. For example, Wednesday at 12:00 translates to 312. Using the phonetic alphabet we can translate 312 into **mitten**.

I have listed below, a word for each of these days and times. You are free to make up your own if you wish.

DAY	**11:00**	**12:00**
Monday	dotted	titan
Tuesday	knotted	antenna
Wednesday	matted	mitten
Thursday	rotate	rotten
Friday	lighted	Aladdin
Saturday	cheated	jitney
Sunday	cadet	kitten

Let's memorize the following appointments:

1. Monday 10:00 Dentist appointment
2. Monday 7:00 P.M. Meet with Bill Schaffer
3. Tuesday 5:15 Call Mrs. Pearlman

Take time to visualize each picture as vividly as possible.

1. See your **dentist** giving you a shot of novocaine in each one of your **toes**. He is going to pull them off your foot!
2. You are **shaving**(Schaffer) your **dog's** whiskers with **black** (P.M.) shaving cream and you are using a dollar **bill** (Bill) to dry his face.
3. You are **nail**ing **pearls** to a **man** who is standing in a pile of **quarters** (twenty-five cent pieces).

Now, when you wake up Monday morning, run through the hours in that day; e.g., tot, tin, tomb, tire, towel, dish, dog, dove, tape, toes, dotted, and titan. When you come to *dog* you will automatically remember your appointment with Bill Schaffer at 7:00 P.M. and when you come to toes you will remember the 10:00 dentist appointment. (You will know it's at 10:00 A.M. and not P.M.)

Run through the hours of the day for Tuesday and see if you can remember your appointment.

Exercise

Practice your peg words for the hours in each day. As you do, visualize each image clearly. Start with Monday and work your way through Sunday. Do this a few times to get comfortable with the system. Now make up a list of appointments and memorize them. Don't forget to include quarter-hours in your exercise, the practice will help you prepare for remembering *real* meetings and scheduled events.

CHAPTER 15

BIRTHDAYS & ANNIVERSARIES

To memorize a person's birthday or anniversary you must link the *month*, *day*, and *event* (birthday or anniversary) to the *person*. We shall handle months as follows:

January	confetti (symbolizes new year)
February	heart (symbolizes Valentine's Day)
March	marching band
April	shower
May	may pole
June	graduation cap
July	fireworks
August	a gust of wind
September	school house (children return to school)
October	witch on broom (Halloween)
November	turkey
December	Santa Claus

Take a couple of minutes to learn the month translations.

Let's suppose you wish to remember that your wife's birthday is July 25th. You might link **fireworks** (July), to **nail** (the peg word for 25), to your wife and a birthday cake. (I chose birthday cake to represent birthday. You can use whatever reminds *you* of a birthday.) Picture your **wife nail**ing **fireworks** (instead of candles) to a **birthday cake**! See that crazy image clearly in your mind and you'll remember her birthday.

Now, if you wish to remember the year she was born, simply translate and add it to the fantasy. Suppose she were born in 1948. Roof is the peg word for 48. (You only need to translate 48; the century is evident.) Now picture your **wife nail**ing **fireworks** to a **birthday cake** as she stands on the **roof** of your house! That takes care of the day, month, year, person, and event all in one crazy picture.

NOTE: *Whenever you link the year into your image, you must do it in a way that it won't be confused with the day. For example; Suppose your grandmother's birthday was October 6, 1914. That translates to **witch** for October, **shoe** for 6 (the day), and **tire** for 14 (the year). When you decode that fantasy, you might mistakenly think her birthday was October 14, 1906 instead of October 6, 1914! To avoid any confusion, picture the person standing on the year (In this case, she would be standing on a tire [14].)*

To make it all clear, lets link grandmother to her birthday. Imagine grandmother *standing* on a giant **tire** throwing a **birthday cake** (lit candles and all) at a **witch** that is flying by on a **shoe** (instead of a broom). In decoding this little fantasy, witch gives us the month (October), tire gives us the year (19**14**), and shoe gives us the day, 6. We know that 14 is the year and not the day because she was standing on it! We also know it was your grandmothers *birthday* because we saw her throwing a *birthday cake* at the witch.

Keep in mind, it took 29 words for me to describe that fantasy but it only takes one picture to see it.

Memorize an anniversary the same way you would memorize a birthday, only substitute a ring (or any appropriate image) for birthday cake. The ring will remind you that the occasion is an anniversary.

CHAPTER 16

THE ALPHABET SYSTEM

The "Alphabet" system is the last peg system I will teach you. It serves not only as a peg list but as a way to "picture" letters. It is similar to the "Number-Rhyme" system and is as easy to use. Each peg is formed by selecting a word that starts with the *sound* of a letter. For example, you might use *cake* to represent the letter K and you might use *elephant* to represent the letter L. Notice that cake doesn't start with the letter K nor does elephant start with the letter L; that's ok because it's the *sound* we're interested in, not the letter. ("Lucky," would be an incorrect choice to represent the letter L.) As with other peg systems, each peg-word should form a picture. You can make up your own "Alphabet" pegs or use the ones I've listed below.

THE ALPHABET IMAGES
A   Abe
B   Bee
C   Sea
D   Deed
E   Easel

THE ALPHABET IMAGES

F   Effervescence (alka-seltzer)
G   Jeep
H   H-bomb
I   Eye
J   Jay bird
K   Cake
L   Elephant
M   M&M's
N   End (as in rear end)
O   Oboe
P   Pea
Q   Queue
R   Arch
S   Eskimo
T   Tea
U   U-boat
V   VD
W   W.C. Fields
X   X-ray
Y   Wife
Z   Zebra

Write, next to the letters below, your choices for the "Alphabet pegs."

"Alphabet" Pegs

A
B
C
D
E
F

"Alphabet" Pegs

G
H
I
J
K
L
M
N
O
P
Q
R
S
T
U
V
W
X
Y
Z

You now have a way to "picture" any letter; e.g., I = **eye**, Z = **zebra** and so on. The "Alphabet" system will come in handy when you need to memorize a code number that includes numbers and letters; e.g., model numbers, licence plate numbers, etc.

To memorize a code number that includes letters, simply translate the numbers and letters into pictures—then link the pictures in a crazy, nonsensical way. To avoid confusing "letter-words" with "number-words," you should cover the "letter-words" with tar. For example, the code 14S99742 can be translated to tire (14), Eskimo (S), and popcorn (99742). Picture yourself throwing a huge **tire** at an **Eskimo** that is covered with hot tar. He is eating a giant bag of **popcorn**. You know that "Eskimo" means S and not 073 (which is the number translation for Eskimo) because he is covered in tar. The tar tells you that the word should translate to a letter, not a number.

Take some time to familiarize yourself with the "Alphabet" pegs. Say them out loud A-Abe, B-Bee, C-Sea and so on. Vividly picture each image as you say it.

After you learn the "Alphabet" pegs, memorize a list of 26 items. Be sure to use the "Memory-Aids." Choose letters randomly and see if you can remember what items you linked to them.

CHAPTER 17

THE PLAYING-CARD SYSTEM

The "Playing-Card" system will enable you to remember the order of an entire deck of cards!

Normally, playing-cards are difficult to remember because they are *intangible* things. We can make them easy to remember by associating them with *tangible* things. As we did with numbers, we will give each card a picture. Once a card can be pictured, it can be associated via the link or the peg.

Whether you are interested in cards or not, I recommend learning this system. You can use the system to exercise your mind. Mental exercise is to memory, what weight lifting is to muscles. Just like muscles, your brain needs to be stretched if you wish to keep it in tip-top shape. Whenever you exercise your brain you are expanding your creative powers.

The System

Each card-word will begin with the first letter of its suit; e.g., C, H, S, D—for Clubs, Hearts Spades, and Diamonds.

The next consonant sound in the word will represent the *value* of the card. Therefore, the word **sock** would represent the 7 of spades. Sock begins with a "s" (Spades) and is followed by the consonant sound "k" (7). The card-word for the 5 of clubs is **coal**. Coal begins with "c" (Clubs) and is followed by the consonant sound "l" (5). We will give "aces" a value of 1; therefore **cat** = AC; **hat** = AH; **suit** = AS; and **date** = AD. We will give "tens" a value of 0; **case** = 10C; **hose** = 10H; **sauce** = 10S; and **dose** = 10D. We'll deal with court cards next; but before we do, take a minute to digest what we've covered.

We will think of jacks as 11, and queens as 12; therefore **cadet** = JC; **headed** = JH; **seeded** = JS; and **deadwood** = JD. **Cotton** = QC; **heathen** = QH; **satin** = QS; and **detain** = QD.

Kings will use the suit words alone; e.g., Clubs, Hearts, Spades, and Diamonds. Therefore, **club** = KC; **heart** = KH; **spade** = KS; and **diamond** = KD.

CARD-WORD IMAGES

Clubs	Hearts	Spades	Diamonds
A C - cat	A H - hat	A S - suit	A D - date
2C - can	2H - hen	2S - sun	2D - dune
3C - comb	3H - hem	3S - sum	3D - dam
4C - car	4H - hare	4S - sewer	4D - door
5C - coal	5H - hail	5S - sail	5D - doll
6C - cash	6H - hash	6S - sash	6D - dish
7C - cake	7H - hog	7S - sock	7D - dog
8C - cuff	8H - hoof	8S - safe	8D - dove
9C - cup	9H - hoop	9S - soap	9D - dab
10C - case	10H - hose	10S - sauce	10D - dose
J C - cadet	J H - headed	J S - seeded	J D - deadwood
Q C - cotton	Q H - heathen	Q S - satin	Q D - detain
K C - club	K H - heart	K S - spade	K D - diamond

The previous list contains a card-word for each of the 52 cards. You may use them or make up your own. Some of the card-words I have chosen do not form pictures in themselves so you must use a symbolic picture to represent them. For example, **seeded** (JS) could be thought of as a freshly tilled garden; **dab** (9D) could be pictured as a squeeze of toothpaste; **dose** (10D) could be thought of as a bottle of pills; and so on.

Now that you understand the system, you must *practice* it. (There's a difference between understanding and knowing.) The best way to practice is with a deck of cards. You might want to print the appropriate card-word on the back of each card then test yourself as follows: Run through the deck and call out the card-word for each card you see. Now flip the deck over and call out the card value as you look at each card-word. *Take some time to learn the card-words before continuing on.*

Exercise

As you read the following story, picture each image as vividly as you can:

There is a **dove** flying over head with a bar of **soap** in it's mouth. The soap falls and lands in a giant **cup**. A **dog** comes along and starts chewing on the soap. A **cat** dressed in a **satin** dress hits the dog over the head with a **club**. It starts to **hail** so the cat jumps into a **sewer** and lands on an old **doll**.

You have just memorized ten cards! Prove it to yourself by thinking through the story and saying each card-word out loud. If you know the system, you remembered the cards.

Making up crazy stories is fun. Let your imagination go wild! Take five cards and make up your own story. The more you do it the easier it becomes.

Pegging cards

We can use the "Major" pegs to memorize an entire deck of cards in and out of order—an impressive feat to say the least. All you need to do is link each card with a "Major" peg. Let's try it with ten cards: Imagine rubbing **cake** all over your **tie**. Picture a **hog** with a long grey beard(**Noah**). Your **ma** is throwing all her **cash** out the window. Your **door** is a giant piece of **rye** bread. There is a police officer(**law**) directing traffic with a **spade**. You are **comb**ing your hair with a **shoe**. You see a giant **key dive** off a diving board. Your foe makes you mad so you lock him in a **safe**. You are using a huge **diamond** to cut a piece of **pie**. You are stirring hot **sauce** with your **toes**.

If you vividly pictured each one of those silly images, then you know the ten cards in and out of order. If I asked you what the third card was you would think ma and see her throwing **cash** out the window—you would know it's the 6C. If I asked you for the ninth card you would say king of diamonds because you saw yourself cutting a pie with a huge diamond; **diamond** stands for one thing only, King of Diamonds.

Try recalling the eight remaining cards on your own.

THE MANGLE TECHNIQUE

There are many card games that require you remember discards; e.g., bridge, gin rummy, canasta, and so on. With the "Mangle" technique, you can remember discards with ease. All you must do is picture the card-word (for the discard) and mangle it in some way. For example, if the 6D was thrown, picture a "broken" **dish**. Dish is the card-word for the 6D—We mangled it by picturing it broken. If the AS is thrown, picture a badly torn **suit**. Suit is the card-word for AS and we mangled it by picturing it torn. Whenever you wish to remember if a card was discarded, simply picture it. If the image you see is "mangled" it was discarded; if the image is intact, it wasn't.

This method works like a charm. Try it with the following exercise:

Exercise

Remove the 2 thru Ace (of one suit) from the deck and set the rest of the cards aside. (Your packet should consist of 13 cards.) Shuffle the packet thoroughly. Without looking, remove one card from the packet. Now mangle the 12 remaining card-pictures as we did in the examples above. When you are finished, mentally review the card-word images for the suit you chose. (Start with the 2 and work your way up.) When you see an image that hasn't been mangled you will know the missing card! (You couldn't have mangled it because it was missing from the packet.) Turn the removed card over to see that you were correct.

Impress your friends with the following memory feat: Have someone shuffle a deck of cards. Let that person remove five or six cards from the deck. Now, have him call out the remaining cards. As he does, visualize the card-images and mangle them. When he has finished, *mentally review* the card-images and call out the card for each image that isn't mangled. (To avoid any confusion, review the cards in specific order. You might do it in alphabetical order; e.g., Ace through K of **C**lubs; Ace - K of **D**iamonds; Ace - K of **H**earts; and Ace - K of **S**pades.) The cards you called out will prove to be the missing cards.

At first, the "Playing-Card" system might seem a little difficult. In time, like any other system, it will become second-nature. All it takes is a little effort. If you enjoy cards, put forth the effort and you will be greatly rewarded.

CHAPTER 18

CURING ABSENTMINDEDNESS

Absentmindedness means absentness of mind. If your mind is focused on something other than what you are doing, you are being "absent-minded."

Forgetfulness and absentmindedness are two different things. In order to forget something, you must know it in the first place. (You can't forget something you don't know.) If you have ever found yourself saying "I forgot where I put my keys," you can be sure that you didn't forget where you put them; you just didn't *remember* where you put them in the first place. Your mind was focused elsewhere when you laid them down—you were absent-minded.

Think of absentmindedness as "*Inattention*." If you pay attention to what you are doing, you can't be absent-minded—your mind is *present* when you focus it on what you are doing.

Association

You can force yourself to pay attention by using *association*. Association, like all other memory techniques, forces

129

original awareness. When you are aware of something, you can remember it.

You've just arrived home from work. As you open your door, the phone rings. You set your keys down on a chair as you rush to answer the phone. The next morning you look for your keys in the place where you normally keep them but they're not there! You search the house for 20 minutes and finally find your keys on the chair; you wonder how in the world they got there.

You could have avoided all that unnecessary searching if you had associated the keys with the chair as you layed them on it. Then, thinking of the keys would have reminded you of where you put them. You might have pictured the **keys** exploding the **chair** as you layed them down. That ridiculous picture would have *forced* you to pay attention—you'd have remembered exactly where they were. Take a second to focus your attention—you'll save a lot of time in the long run.

If you take off your ring to wash your hands, see yourself wearing a bar of **soap** instead of a **ring**. You can make the association as you wash. The next time you think of your ring you will see a bar of soap on your finger and remember where you left it. You'll remember because you forced yourself to pay attention.

If you place your glasses in the glove box of your car, see yourself wearing eye-**gloves** instead of eye-**glasses**. Form the picture as you place the glasses in the glove box. I guarantee you'll remember where they are the next time you need them. **NOTE:** *Whenever you associate, use your "memory-aids."*

How many times have you hidden valuable items in a place where nobody could find them, including yourself? We can use association to solve that problem also.

Let's say you have an expensive diamond ring that you

only wear on special occasions. You want to keep it in an inconspicuous place so you rest it on a pipe underneath your kitchen sink. As you put it there, see a picture of the diamond cutting right through the pipe causing thousands of gallons of water to flood your kitchen floor! *If you try this method you will see that it works beautifully.*

Reminders'

Let's suppose you want to remember to bring a book to work with you. Associate *book* with the last thing you'll be sure to notice when you leave your house. You might picture your **door** as a giant **book**. When you open the door to leave the house, it will remind you of the book. If you want to be double sure to remember the book, associate it to your car. See yourself driving a **book** to work instead of a **car**—see people looking at you in amazement as you drive by on a book! (If the door doesn't remind you, the car will.)

Say you want to remember to buy eggs on your way home from work. All you have to do is associate *eggs* with any landmark that you have to pass on your way home. Maybe the landmark is a statue of an eagle. Picture the **eagle** hatching a giant **egg**; or see eggs smashed all over it. Now, when you see the eagle on your way home you'll remember to stop and buy eggs.

Many people forget things in the oven or on the stove and end up ruining pots and pans or even starting a fire. It's easy to forget a pot of boiling water on the stove if you are in another room watching television. The solution is to place a frying pan (or similar utensil) on top of the TV—it will remind you of the boiling water.

Have you ever gone into the kitchen to get something out of the refrigerator and forgotten what it was you wanted?

You open the door and stare. . . . Next time, make an association as soon as you think of what it is you want. If you're sitting in your living room and decide you would like an apple, picture thousands of **apples** falling out of the **refrigerator** as you open the door. You won't forget!

Have you ever spent an evening away from home worrying about whether or not you locked the door? Next time, when you're locking the door, see yourself locking it with your teeth! Feel and taste the key in your mouth. You won't be plagued with that problem ever again.

If you ever wake up in the middle of the night with a brilliant idea, toss a nearby object on your bedroom floor. Then, make an association between that object and your idea. When you wake up in the morning you will see the out-of-place object and it will remind you of your idea.

Train yourself to be more aware

Through all our senses, our mind receives millions of messages each day. Fortunately, we have an innate ability to block out information we don't need and keep only what we do. We'd go mad if we were consciously aware of every message our brain received. On the other hand, most of us block out more than we should—we are not aware of as much as we could be. The chapter on "People and Names" is a testimonial to how unaware we are of peoples faces, even though we see them everyday. Many other things that exist in our everyday-lives go just as unnoticed. Our task is to start noticing them.

We can sharpen our sense of awareness by paying closer attention to the things that surround us. Look at things in more detail than you normally do. Be aware of shapes, colors, and textures. By doing so, you will enhance your awareness in general. This form of mental exercise will have a positive effect on the way you remember. At first you must make a conscious effort to do this but after a while you will do it automatically. Don't forget; in order to remember something you must be aware of it!

CHAPTER 19

STUDY TECHNIQUES

Studies show that within a 24 hour period we forget almost 80% of what we read or hear. That translates into 48 minutes of wasted time per-hour of study, or, 8-hours of wasted time per ten hours of study. Either way, it adds up to be an enormous waste of time.

On the other hand, we can use proper study techniques to help us increase our productivity up to 80%! That means we can remember in 1 hour what would normally take us 5. Using proper study techniques make sense—the advantages are obvious.

Understanding vs. Remembering

We assume that just because we understand something we will remember it. That isn't true! Understanding and remembering are two different things. You can read book after book nodding your head saying "I see, uh huh, yep, I get it," but you won't remember much of what you read. The natural instinct is to keep reading as you understand what you read—figuring you're on a roll, keep going. That's the wrong way to do it. Why do you think most people need to re-read books? In time, your recall-ability gets progressively worse unless you stop to give your mind a rest.

Recall

Under normal circumstances (assuming we understand the material being presented) we seem to recall more from the first and last parts of a learning period; information falling in-between is usually less recallable. The following graph illustrates this:

2-HOUR LEARNING PERIOD

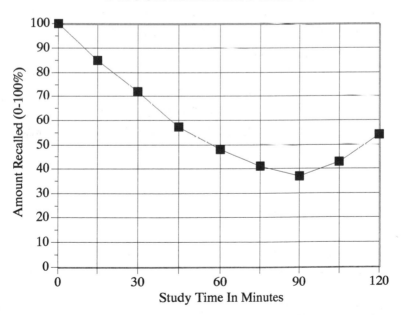

Immediately following a learning period, our ability to recall is at maximum level. Recall then declines sharply in the time there-after. (See graph below)

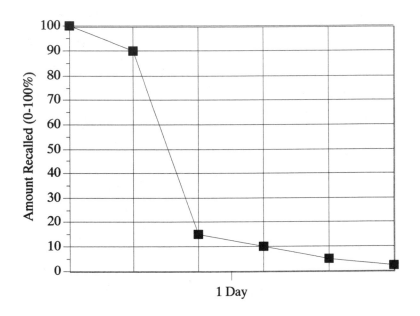

We can conclude that *review* is essential immediately following a learning period, for that is the point when we remember the most. Reviewing helps to plant the information firmly in the memory, therefore our recall level will remain high over a longer period of time.

Also, we can increase our recall-ability if we break learning sessions down into smaller learning periods; e.g., a two hour study session could be broken down into 3 forty-minute sessions, or, 6 twenty-minute sessions. In doing so, we will have more beginning and ending *peaks* and less slope in between. We also will be reviewing more often; e.g., (six learning periods would require six reviews, one after each period.) The result will be a much higher level of recall. (See graph below)

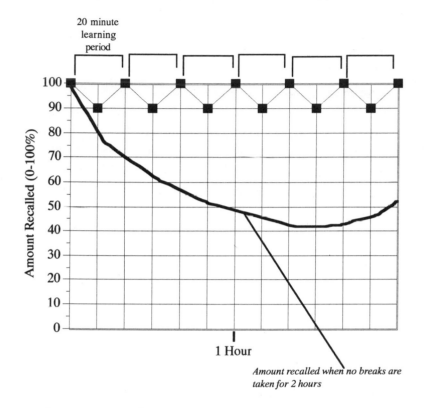

Amount recalled when no breaks are taken for 2 hours

The graph above shows that upon completing 6 twenty-minute learning sessions we have 12 "beginning" and "ending" peaks" and 6 review periods. **NOTE:** *You should take ten minutes to review a 1 hour learning session. Review a 20 minute session for approximately three minutes.*

Reviewing after a learning period will help you retain information for approximately 24 hours. It is near the end of this 24 hour period that you should review again. The second review should help you retain information for approximately one week. At that point you should review the information again. One month after that you should review once more, then the information will be *knowledge*. Keep in mind, each review session should take only 2 - 4 minutes.

Note-taking

Proper note taking will enable a productive review. Your notes must contain key-words or phrases that will trigger your memory to recall the information. Notes should be taken throughout a learning period. At the end of each period you will have a collection of words and phrases to use for review. At the end of an over-all learning session, you should revise your notes by weeding out unnecessary words. Revising your notes serves as a concentrated review of the information and results in fewer, more potent, key-words.

Key-words don't necessarily have to be words that the author or speaker used, they can be any words that remind you of what is being read or said. Any key-word or phrase you choose is fine as long as it does its job in triggering the proper information.

Throughout high-school and college we are taught to take notes in *outline* format as follows:

```
1. Group One
    a.
    b.
            i
    c.
            i
            ii
2. Group Two
    a.
            i
            ii
    b.
    c.              (etc.)
```

Outline format is *linear* and doesn't lend itself to be easily modified; For example, if you later wished to add something to "Group One," you couldn't, because it has already been structured. You'd have to squeeze words into small spaces or erase and redo.

The brain doesn't think in a *linear* fashion; it needs to jump around from idea to idea as it forms an over-all picture or understanding of all elements involved. It would be much better to use an *open* style of notation; one that will allow us to jump from idea to idea and enable us to slot in new information wherever and whenever we need to. Following, is a *basic* example of open-ended notating:

Notice the *main* idea is placed in the center. The more

important ideas are closer to the center and the less important ideas are further away. Each key concept can be easily recognized because of its closeness to the center. In the linear outline format, each key concept is separated by a list of subordinate ideas; this makes for slower review. If you wished to add more information to the outline above you could do it easily. This type of outline will allow the brain to grasp the overall picture of the information far more quickly. Also notice the use of pictures. Our brain thinks in pictures, remember? It makes sense to use pictures in our note taking. In fact, we should use color and dimension too. Color, dimension and pictures are all *right-brain* functions. We should use them in harmony with our logical more linear *left-brain*. In this way we will be using the power of our *whole* brain!

Exercise

Take out a piece of paper and draw an open-ended outline, as we did above, using this chapter as your subject matter. Start with the main idea in the center and add the key concepts and relative information as you go. Remember to keep the more important ideas closer to the center and use branches to connect relative information to them. Try to use one key-word per branch. This will force you to think the material through and will make memorization easier. Use pictures and colored markers to enhance the effectiveness of the outline. You should do this exercise as you review this chapter. Start now.

Exercise

Using your favorite peg system, link each primary keyword from the outline you just made (the words closest to the center) to the pegs on your list. Do this now. To recall the material in this chapter simply think of each of the pegs that you linked your key-words to. The pegs will remind you of your key-words and your key-words will trigger the information. You have in effect memorized the whole chapter!

This form of note-taking might feel awkward at first; that's because you've been using linear outlining your whole life. Linear forms of note-taking are useful when you need to remember sequentially listed information. Use linear outlining only when it's appropriate. *Once you get used to the open style, you won't want to go back.*

Use the methods in this chapter whenever you read to *learn*. Take breaks every 20 - 40 minutes as we've discussed. Give yourself time to absorb the information you've learned. The same principles apply to lectures, only with lectures you don't have the privilege to stop every half hour to review. That's where being fluent with open-ended outlining pays off. Start using these techniques immediately. If you're willing to spend precious hours reading or listening, you might as well make the most of them!

CHAPTER 20

MEMORIZING MAGAZINES & BOOKS

Magazines

Memorizing magazines is an excellent way to exercise your imagination. It's also a great way to impress your friends with your super-power memory. The object is to link each page of the magazine and its content, to a peg from the "Master" peg-list. Each peg will represent the page number; e.g., tie = page 1; Noah = page 2; ma = page 3; and so on. Now we must form a link between the peg, and 2 or 3 items from the page. (You can choose headlines or pictures.) Let's assume that on the top of the first page is a picture of a man fishing. In the middle of the page is an advertisement for Crest Toothpaste; and near the bottom is a headline that reads, "Man Killed by Bull." Our job is to link **tie** (the peg-word that represents the first page) to **man fishing** to **Crest Toothpaste** to "**Man Killed by Bull.**" Once the link is formed, all you have to do is think **tie** and you'll remember what you linked to it. Let's try it.

Picture yourself **fishing** with your **tie** instead of a fishing pole. See yourself pulling the tie out of the water and there's a fish on the end of it! Now picture yourself using a piece of **crust** (Crest) to brush the fish's teeth! Suddenly, a **bull** comes running by with its horns sticking right through a **man**'s body; the man is dead. The bull grabs your fish as he runs by—(This image will remind you of the headline, "Man Killed by Bull.") On the top of page two you see the headline, "Mailboxes Vandalized." In the middle of the page is a picture of an ice-skater. We must link **Noah** to **"Mailboxes Vandalized"** to **ice-skater**. Picture an old man with a grey beard (Noah) that hangs down past his belt. He is sneaking around in the night smashing **mailboxes** with his cane! A man wearing **ice-skate**s spots him doing this and chases him down the street. You can see sparks flying as he skates after him! (*You would continue through the magazine memorizing each page in the same way.*)

After you memorize the magazine have someone call out a page number. When he does, you will translate the number to it's "Master" peg-word and instantly remember your preposterous link as follows: Assuming he called out page 2 you would think **Noah**—(represents page 2) which reminds you of the old man with the gray beard—(**Noah**) smashing mail-boxes with his cane. That would give you the headline "**Mailboxes Vandalized.**" (Your true memory will tell you the headline, "Mailboxes Vandalized.") You would then be reminded of the **ice-skater** chasing the old man down the street.

Exercise

Memorize a current magazine (preferably one with a lot of illustrations). Once you've memorized it, go back and look through it again, this time pay more attention to detail.

For example, if you see a picture of a car, notice the color and make. Don't try to memorize the color or make just be aware of it—your true memory will do the rest for you. This process will help lock the images firmly into your memory. After your second look, test yourself or have a friend test you. Have him call out any page. When he does, make your associations and proceed to describe the contents.

SUGGESTION: *You can practice memorizing magazines as you wait in a dentist or doctor's office. (There are always a few magazines laying around.) Why not take advantage of the time you'd otherwise waste waiting?*

Books

Memorizing a book is the most rewarding memory experience of all. Reading a book more than once usually isn't necessary when you apply the "Study Techniques" taught in chapter 19 and the memory systems taught throughout this book.

My favorite book on human relations is "How To Win Friends & Influence People" by Dale Carnegie. (If you don't have it, get it— everybody who's anybody has read it.) The book contains many principles that must be learned and practiced. If you don't remember them, you can't use them—if you don't use them, they don't work! The point is, if you wish to take advantage of this fantastic book you must *memorize* the principles. This is a perfect example of a book that should be memorized.

To memorize a book, all you must do is pick out a key word or two from each paragraph on each page. (Make sure the key-words you choose will trigger your memory to remember what the paragraph is saying.) After you choose the key words for each paragraph on the page, link them (as we did above) to the "Major" peg-list. **NOTE:** *In chapter 22, I will show you how to instantly expand the "Major" peg-list. The extra pegs will accommodate all your key-words.*

Exercise

Use the techniques taught in this chapter and the "Study Techniques" taught in chapter 19 to memorize a chapter from your favorite book.

CHAPTER 21

MEMORIZING SPEECHES

There is a right way and a wrong way to memorize a speech. The wrong way is to memorize it word for word. Speeches delivered in this manner are unnatural and have a phony quality to them—they're not as *believable*. Listeners will pay less attention to what you're saying and more attention to *how* you're saying it. If a speech is so critical that no word can be out of place, it should be read.

The purpose of a speech is to communicate a message. The message should be supported by a number of ideas that directly or indirectly relate to it. The right way to memorize a speech is to memorize the *ideas* and the order in which you wish to present them. Assuming you are familiar with the subject on which you are speaking, all you will need is the idea to remind you of what you wish to say. A speech delivered in this way has a spontaneous energetic quality.

After the speech is written, identify and list key-words. (Each key-word will represent an idea.) Now link each key-word, in succession, to the "Loci" pegs. To deliver the speech, imagine your "Loci" pegs. Each peg will remind you of the idea you linked to it, and each idea will remind you of what you want to say. In this way, your speech will follow the logical order in which it was written.

The "Loci" system is used because the pegs are items in your home—You are comfortable in your home and thinking of it will help you relax as you make your speech. Also, even under pressure, the pegs in the "Loci" system are *easy* to remember because they are a part of your everyday life.

Once you've memorized your key-words, practice delivering the speech. Stand up in the middle of your living room and go through it from beginning to end. Let the "Loci" pegs remind you of your key-words. The key-words will trigger your ideas and you'll be off and running.

HINT: When writing your speech you might consider drawing an outline of what you wish to convey. The open-ended outline format taught in chapter 19 is ideal for this. It will allow you to add ideas as you think of them. Each idea will branch off the main message which is written in the middle of the page. If you wish to add a subordinate idea to one of your primary ideas, simply branch off it. Once you have written down all your ideas, you should number them in an order you wish to convey them. Then you can link them to your "Loci" peg-list.

You can use this system to remember points you wish to cover in a business meeting or a telephone conversation. The object is to outline (using the open-ended outline format) what you wish to convey (before your meeting or phone call) then memorize each idea using the "Loci" system. Now you'll remember to cover everything you wanted to and you'll express yourself in an organized easy to understand manner. (This technique is handy *especially* in pressure situations.)

CHAPTER 22

HOW TO INSTANTLY EXPAND ANY PEG-LIST

We will use the "Number-Shape" system to demonstrate how you can instantly expand the capacity of a peg-list. The same methods will apply to any other peg-list. For purposes of demonstration I will use my list—substitute your own list if it's different from mine.

"NUMBER-SHAPE" PEGS

Pencil
Swan
Breasts
Sailboat
Hook
Cherry
Cliff
Hour Glass
Golf Club
Bat and Ball

148

All you have to do is visualize each peg as if it were made out of "**rubber**." Here's what you should see:

"RUBBER-NUMBER-SHAPE" PEGS

Rubber-Pencil
Rubber-Swan
Rubber-Breasts
Rubber-Sailboat
Rubber-Hook
Rubber-Cherry
Rubber-Cliff
Rubber-Hour Glass
Rubber-Golf Club
Rubber-Bat and Ball

Picture each peg as vividly as you can!

That's it! You can use this new list of pegs just as you would use any other peg-list. Don't worry about confusing the "Rubber" pegs with the regular Number-Shape pegs, you won't. Prove that to yourself by doing the following exercise.

Exercise
On the following page is a list of twenty items. Use your "Number-Shape" peg-list to memorize the first ten; then use the "**Rubber** -Number-Shape" peg-list to memorize items 11-20. Be sure to use your memory aids and form crystal clear images as you link.

ITEM LIST

1. **Sandwich**	11. **Ear**
2. **Basketball**	12. **Coffee Table**
3. **Sock**	13. **House**
4. **Couch**	14. **Desert**
5. **Note Pad**	15. **Car**
6. **Wrist Watch**	16. **Knife**
7. **Fence**	17. **Hand**
8. **Hunger**	18. **Common Pin**
9. **Sheep**	19. **Anger**
10. **Pine Tree**	20. **Lipstick**

Without looking at the list above, fill in the correct item next to each of the numbered spaces below and on the following page.

1. _____	11. _____
2. _____	12. _____
3. _____	13. _____
4. _____	14. _____
5. _____	15. _____
6. _____	16. _____
7. _____	17. _____
8. _____	18. _____
9. _____	19. _____
10. _____	20. _____

20. _____   10. _____
19. _____   9. _____
18. _____   8. _____
17. _____   7. _____
16. _____   6. _____
15. _____   5. _____
14. _____   4. _____
13. _____   3. _____
12. _____   2. _____
11. _____   1. _____

15. _____   11. _____
 4. _____   14. _____
 9. _____   19. _____
 5. _____   18. _____
10. _____   3. _____
12. _____   13. _____
 8. _____   17. _____
20. _____   2. _____
 1. _____   16. _____
 7. _____   6. _____

As I have stated above, this method can be applied to any peg-list including the "Master" peg-list. If you've learned all 100 "Master" pegs, you can instantly double them to 200 pegs! All you need to do is picture them as follows:

rubber-tie
rubber-beard (Noah)
rubber-ma
rubber-rye   etc.

Are you ready for more exciting news? You can triple or quadruple any peg list by adding a different modifier to the pegs; e.g.,

Modifier	*Peg*
Glass	Pencil
Glass	Swan
Glass	Breasts
Glass	Sailboat . . .
Or	
Cardboard	Pencil
Cardboard	Swan
Cardboard	Breasts. . . and so on.

The only way to convince yourself that this method works is to try it in the following exercise.

Exercise

Make up a list of 30 items and memorize it using your "**Rubber**-Number-Shape", "**Glass**-Number-Shape," and "**Cardboard**-Number-Shape" peg-lists. **NOTE:** *Get a vivid picture of each peg as you link it to an item.*

Use your imagination and make up your own modifiers. Be sure and take the time to see each peg clearly. When you've established four or five of your own modifiers, decide on the order in which you'll use them. For example, if you wish to use modified "Major" peg-lists you might use them as follows:

Unmodified pegs	represent	1-100
Cardboard pegs	represent	101-200
Glass pegs	represent	201-300
Rubber pegs	represent	301-400 etc.

In the previous example I used the modifiers in alphabetical order; e.g., **C**ardboard, **G**lass, and **R**ubber. Now I can remember which "hundred" each of them represent.

This easy and powerful way to expand peg lists should not be taken lightly; it WORKS! Please give it a chance, you'll be glad you did.

CHAPTER 23

MEMORIZING THE CALENDAR

Here is a system by which you can figure out, almost instantly, the day of the week for any date in a year. You first must link the date of the first Monday of each month to its respective month. With this date you can figure out any other day in the month. Following are a list of dates on which the first Monday of each month fall in the year 1990:

Month	Date 1st Monday falls on
January	1
February	5
March	5
April	2
May	7
June	4
July	2
August	6
September	3
October	1
November	5
December	3

We see that the first Monday in January falls on the 1st so we must link 1 to January. (We will use picture words to represent the months as we did in the chapter on "Birthdays & Anniversaries." See list below.) Our picture word for January is *confetti*. We can link 1 to confetti by picturing a man cutting his **tie** (represents 1) into millions of tiny pieces of **confetti**. He throws the pieces up in the air and yells "Happy New Year." The first Monday in February falls on the 5th—Our picture word for February is *heart* and our picture for the number 5 is *law*. We can link heart to law by picturing a traffic officer (**law**) stopping each person that drives by and checking their **heart** with a stethoscope.

Finish linking each date to its respective month. Below are the picture words for each month:

January	confetti
February	heart
March	marching band
April	shower
May	may pole
June	graduation cap
July	fireworks
August	a gust of wind
September	school house (children return to school)
October	witch on broom (Halloween)
November	turkey
December	Santa Claus

Now that you've memorized the dates it will be easy for you to figure out the day in the week for any date in the year. Assume we wish to figure out the day of the week for January 9th. You would think **confetti** for January and you would see the picture of a man cutting his **tie** into confetti.

This would tell you that the first Monday of the month falls on the 1st. A simple calculation would tell you that the 9th of January falls on a Tuesday. (By adding 7 to 1 we get 8—the 8th falls on a Monday therefore, the 9th is a Tuesday.)

Exercise

Using the system you just learned, figure out the days for the following dates:

May 2nd
June 16th
August 3rd
July 22nd
September 9th
February 15th

BIBLIOGRAPHY/ RECOMMENDED READING

Bienstock, Eric M. *Success Through Better Memory*.

Buzan, Tony. *Make The Most Of Your Mind*. New York: Simon & Schuster Inc., 1984.

Buzan, Tony. *Use Both Sides Of Your Brain*. New York: E. P. Dutton, 1983.

Buzan, Tony. *Use Your Perfect Memory*. New York: E. P. Dutton, 1984.

Ebbinghaus, Hermann. *Memory A Contribution To Experimental Psychology*. New York: Dover Publications, Inc., 1964.

Edwards, Betty. *Drawing On The Artist Within*. New York: Simon & Shuster, Inc., 1987.

Edwards, Betty. *Drawing On The Right Side Of The Brain*. Los Angeles: Jeremy P. Tarcher, Inc., 1989.

Furst, Bruno. S*top Forgetting*. New York: Greenberg, 1949.

Harrison, Allen F., and Robert M. Bramson. *The Art Of Thinking*. New York: Berkely Book, 1982.

Kellet, Michael C. *How to Improve Your Memory and Concentration*. New York: Monarch Press, 1977.

Lapp, Danielle C. *Don't Forget!* New York: McGraw-Hill, 1987.

Lorayne, Harry. *Memory Makes Money*. Boston: Little, Brown, 1988.

Lorayne, Harry, and Lucas, Jerry. *The Memory Book*. New York: Ballantine Books, 1974.

Minninger, Joan. *Total Recall*. New York: Pocket Books, 1986.

Murphy, Joseph. *The Power Of Your Subconscious Mind.* New Jersey: Prentice-Hall, 1963.

Robbins, Anthony. *Unlimited Power.* New York: Ballentine Books, 1986.

Roth, David M. *Roth Memory Course*. New York: The Sun Dial Press, 1918.

Slung, Michele. *The Absent-Minded Professor's Memory Book.* New York: Ballantine Books, 1985.

von Oech, Roger. *A Whack On The Side Of The Head: How To Unlock Your Mind For Innovation.* New York: Warner Books, 1983.

Yates, F. A. *The Art Of Memory.* New York: Penguin Books, 1978.

About the Author

Robert Sandstrom is a nationally recognized memory-training expert. His skill-building seminars and workshops for major corporations, sales organizations, government agencies and university schools of business utilize his unprecedented memory-honing techniques. He is frequently in demand as a speaker, lecturer, training consultant and TV-radio guest.

Sandstrom, whose memory mastery was perfected during his years as a celebrated composer/musician, now shows others how to apply these same remarkable methods to improve study skills, retain more of what they learn and command "instant" recall.